The Everyday, Anytime Guide to Prayer

The Everyday, Anytime Guide to Prayer

Walt Kallestad

Augsburg

Minneapolis

THE EVERYDAY, ANYTIME GUIDE TO PRAYER

Cover design: Cindy Cobb-Olson
Inside Design: Kathy McEnaney

Library of Congress Cataloging in Publication Data

Kallestad, Walt P., 1948–
    The everyday, anytime guide to prayer/Walt Kallestad.
        p. cm.
    ISBN 0-8066-2796-4 (alk. paper)
        1. Prayer—Christianity. 2. Prayer—Christianity—Meditations.
    I. Title
    BV210.2.K25 1995
    242'.2—dc20   94-41735
                                                                    CIP

The paper used in this publication meets the minimum requirements of American National Standard for Information Sciences—Permanence of Paper for Printed Library Materials, ANSI Z329.48-1984.   ∞™

Manufactured in the U.S.A.   AF 10-27964

99   98   97   96   3   4   5   6   7   8   9   10

Contents

To my great friend,

personal intercessor,

and teammate at Community Church of Joy,

Bjorn Pedersen.

You are deeply loved and cherished!

---

*I*ntroduction

Prayer Is for Everyone—Every Day, Any Time

———◆———

Lord, teach us to pray . . .
Luke 11:1

Andy Weaver is a bushy-bearded, hard working, down-to-earth, ready-to-laugh guy who doesn't need help from a pillow to play Santa at Christmas. Andy is an avid motorcyclist and looks like everyone's stereotype of a biker, but the power of his heart of gold is more than a match for the power of his Honda Gold Wing℠. "The time I feel closest to God," Andy confides, "is when I'm on my bike. That's how I learned to pray with my eyes open," he chuckles. Andy especially delights in praying while he is on long rides.

Now, cruising down the interstate on a Gold Wing is hardly the place most people think of praying, but the image shows that prayer truly is for everyone—every day and anytime. Prayer, like conversation between friends and family members, is meant to be a natural part of our daily lives. On the job, at home, at school, in our relationships, in our loneliness, in our sorrow and joy, God wants to communicate with us, to hear about us, and to talk with us. Just ask Andy. He'll tell you God was with him when he lost an eye to a drunk with a gun. And through the long days afterward, God answered the many prayers offered by Andy, his family, and his friends.

The Bible tells us God's Son, Jesus, would be called *Emmanuel*, meaning "God with us." Jesus' disciples called him teacher, Lord, and master, titles of respect, admiration, awe, and love. And what did Jesus call his disciples? The disciples had been relating to Jesus as servants relate to a master. But Jesus said, "I do not call you servants any longer, because the servant does not know what the master is doing; but I have called you friends . . ." (John 15:15).

God-with-us calls us "friends." Jesus is our friend as well as our teacher and our only master. And so we will find God with us wherever we are, ready to teach us, help us, and love us through everything that is ordinary and common—or uncommon —in our lives. Prayer is not a series of stopovers on our journey. Prayer is the journey with the One who knows us best, loves us most, and wants to be known by us—as friend.

Maybe a motorcycle seat is not such an odd place, then, to pray!

Chapter 1

Prayer
Expectations

———◆———

Before they call I will answer.
Isaiah 65:24

Expectant prayer opens our eyes
as well as our hands
to perceive and receive God's answers.

1

"Which one of you," the Teacher said, "if you are
expecting an important phone call, will leave your house
and go out into the garage without turning up the ringer
and leaving the door to your house ajar so that you will
hear the call when it comes? Do you not even take your
cordless phone into the back yard so that you can receive
the message? Then I say to you, when you pray keep an
open ear and carry an expectant heart with you, so that
you will hear God's answer when it comes, for God will
surely return your call."

———————◆———————

Our enthusiasm was uncontainable when the doctor
told us we were going to have a baby. Everywhere my
wife and I went, we couldn't wait to tell the good news:
"We're expecting a baby!" Every one of us can be just as
excited and expectant when we pray.

During pregnancy, a woman carries the child within
her while God directs the creation of that new life. It's
much the same with expectant, "pregnant" prayer: we carry the hope of that prayer within us while God works to
bring it to life.

Many people pray but really don't expect anything to
happen. Rather than praying, they are wishing, as in "God,
I wish you would help me," or "You'd better keep your
fingers crossed and pray." But praying and wishing are
complete opposites. Wishing depends on luck. Praying depends on God. Luck is uncertain. God is certain.

One thing that is certain about true prayer is that
God always answers prayer. Sometimes the answer is
"yes" and sometimes the answer is "no." Still other times

the answer is "wait." We can also be certain that the One who answers prayer, our loving God, knows our real needs even better than we do. So God will always answer our prayers in the way that is best for us, even though that may be very different from what we request.

Expectation and answered prayer go together. First, expectation helps us hear God's *answer*. If we pray but don't expect any answer at all, we might not hear what God has to say because we aren't listening anyway. Second, expectation helps us hear *God's* answer. If we pray but expect to hear only the answer we want, we might miss the real answer.

Maybe you've heard the story of a drowning man who prayed for help. The man struggled desperately in deep water, trying to keep his head above water. He cried out in prayer, "God, help me, help me, help me!"

Less than a minute later, a woman in a rowboat came by and offered help. The man said, "No, I'm praying God will help me." One minute later a helicopter flew over and offered a rescue rope. Again the man refused, saying, "No, I'm praying God will help me." Less than a minute later a speedboat pulled up and the driver offered help. Again the man refused. Finally, the man drowned. When he came face to face with God, he demanded to know why God didn't save his life. God responded, "Well, I tried! I sent a rowboat, a helicopter, and a speedboat, but you sent them all away."

How often does our lack of expectation in prayer cause us to miss God's answer? The Bible makes a promise: God answers prayer. "This is the confidence we have in approaching God; that if we ask anything according to his will, he hears us" (1 John 5:14 NIV). We can expect all of our prayers to be answered.

David Logan, a D.A.R.E. police officer, was on a stakeout. Suddenly a man with a rapid-fire pistol appeared and riddled David with bullets. David's partner radioed for help. When the paramedics arrived, David's vital systems had completely shut down. He was given little hope for survival.

By the time David arrived at the hospital, his situation was even worse. After further examination, the doctors informed David's family that there was less than a ten percent chance of his survival. And even if he did survive, David would be paralyzed, and he would certainly never walk again.

Sheila, David's wife, called her pastors and her friends and asked them to pray. They prayed expectantly. The prayers brought encouragement and courage to David and he began the slow recovery process. After months of rehabilitation David revealed his own secret prayer. He had prayed expectantly that one day he would walk out of the hospital. And he did!

Today, God expects to hear from you, and you can expect an answer.

------◆------

Today's Prayer

Dear God, when I pray, help me to expect you to answer, to trust that you will provide the best for my life. Give me new expectations to receive what you are willing, eager, and ready to give. Thank you for always listening to me and understanding my deepest needs. Now I am going to give you my requests. Amen

Growing in Prayer

Write down a need you have. Offer a prayer for that need. Show that you are ready to receive God's answer by holding your empty hands palms up when you pray.

Chapter 2

Prayer Language

---◆---

The Lord accepts my prayer.
Psalm 6:9

Prayer often feels most comfortable
when it has that lived-in look!

2

"*I* really like your new home," commented Sylvan to Laura. Looking around the kitchen, he asked, "Wasn't this one of the model homes in this development?"

"Yes, it was," said Laura, "but we didn't buy it furnished. The interior designer did a beautiful job with it, but it just didn't feel right. We decided we needed to use our own things, whether everything coordinated or not."

Sylvan smiled. "So that's what's different about it, then," he remarked. "I saw this house, too, when it was a model. I liked some of the things the designer had done, but I really like what you've done with it. It feels . . . you know, homey."

"I know what you mean," nodded Laura.

Laura paused, and then added, "You know, deciding how to furnish this house taught me something about self-confidence. I might not know all the latest styles, but I know what feels right to me. And I think it's the same thing when you're praying." She noted Sylvan's puzzled look and went on. "I always thought prayer had to be so formal, but I also felt like I was using someone else's words. There was nothing wrong with those words, but they weren't mine. I never felt 'at home' in my prayer."

"Like living in a model house?" asked Sylvan.

"Exactly," Laura agreed. "It was when I brought 'my own things' into my prayers—myself, really—that I began to feel at home with God."

"You mean I don't have to say things perfectly?" Sylvan grinned. "I don't have to keep God in the living room?"

"Not if you're more comfortable sitting in the kitchen. Wherever your heart is," said Laura, "God will feel welcome, and you'll feel at home, too."

———————◆———————

A friend of mine related this story from her child-hood. When she was nine, her third grade Sunday school teacher asked everyone in the class to write a prayer. The children thoughtfully wrote. The teacher collected the papers, read them, and pronounced my friend's prayer "the best." They closed the class by praying "the best" prayer. My friend said she felt embarrassed and confused. "I was glad that the teacher liked my prayer, but what made mine 'better' than Frank's prayer for his lost dog? Did God choose which prayers to listen to by deciding which sounded 'the best'?"

I could sympathize with my friend's puzzlement. As a teenager, I was afraid to pray out loud because I didn't want to sound stupid. As I listened to all the religious-sounding prayers offered by other Christians, I felt too intimidated to pray out loud. Now that I am a pastor, I am often asked to be the "professional prayer" at both religious and non-religious functions. People seem to assume that I will know the right words to say.

How did the notion that prayer had to sound "religious" ever get started? It's an idea that's been around a long time. Jesus often challenged the religious folks who stood up in public places to flaunt their pious religious platitudes. Jesus saw how empty their words word.

The truth is that, at the heart of the matter, it's the heart that matters. By using language that doesn't really suit us, language that we borrow from someone else, we make it hard to offer prayers of the heart. We tie our heads up with finding the right words, rather than focusing on the real need. Heart expressions expose our deepest emotions and desires. Yes, the Bible tells us that God knows the intentions of our heart. Even so, when we express our hearts, our prayer touches the very heart of God and opens us to God's guidance and healing.

Not long ago I participated in a prayer group at church. In my group were two very religious people and one nonreligious person. As we prayed, the religious people tried to sound more spiritual than God, and I'll admit their prayers did sound profound. When the nonreligious person prayed, on the other hand, she simply said, "God, my life's a mess. I feel like I'm driving into a ditch. Please help me. Amen."

Wow! When I heard that simple expression of the heart, I knew exactly what that woman was feeling. This woman's prayer moved my heart. I felt an intimate connection with God and with one of God's special creations.

Jesus used prayer language that was simple, honest, heartfelt, and fresh. He encouraged us when we pray to say:

"Our Father in heaven, hallowed be your name, your kingdom come, your will be done on earth as it is in heaven. Give us today our daily bread. Forgive us our debts, as we also have forgiven our debtors. And lead us not into temptation, but deliver us from the evil one" (Matthew 6:9b-13).

Today let's encourage each other to use prayer language that simply says what on our hearts.

Today's Prayer

Dear God, help me rise out of language ruts and rituals that keep me from exposing my heart. When I pray, silently or out loud, teach me to express the intimacy that we enjoy with one another. Amen

Growing in Prayer

Write a prayer using your own words.

Chapter 3

Prayer
Triggers

---◆---

Pray in the Spirit at all times.
Ephesians 6:18

Live on the "pray as you go" plan!

3

Marilyn and Tony walked together through the automatic door into the building where they worked, each clutching full coffee cups, lunch bags, briefcases, and newspapers.

"That's what I need in my life," sighed Marilyn.

"Another arm?" quipped Tony.

"No," laughed Marilyn, "though that would come in handy. I mean in my prayer life. I wish I could be like that automatic door."

"What do you mean?" Tony asked.

"If someone asks me to, I'll pray for them," explained Marilyn, "kind of like a door that opens when it's pushed. But I usually just remember a quick prayer in the morning, and at the end of the day I realize that was the only time I prayed all day long. I want to change that."

"So where does the automatic door fit in?" Tony asked.

"Well, think about how they work," prompted Marilyn. "They have a sensor, and as soon as the sensor detects someone, it triggers a circuit that opens the door."

"But what does this have to do with prayer?" Tony asked.

"Well, I think prayer was meant to be like an automatic door," continued Marilyn, "opening freely all day in response to needs. That's what I want: sensors to recognize needs and signal me to pray."

"Maybe we should start by asking God to make us sensitive to the world around us," Tony suggested. "We already have the eyes and ears to pick up the signals."

"I'm sure you're right. And no doubt what unlocks the door in the first place is the desire to begin," Marilyn concluded. "This might not be so hard after all."

My prayer life was in the pits. I knew that prayer was important but I just didn't have time to pray. I was forced to be creative. I figured I had about 30 minutes in the morning when I could pray while I was jogging. I decided to give it a "trial run."

The next morning as I jogged my first step I started to pray. Things were going well until for some reason, I closed my eyes—maybe because my Sunday school teacher always told us to close our eyes when we prayed. BAM! I tripped and wiped out, ripping my shirt, my shorts, and my skin. Embarrassed, I got up and shuffled home.

Bleeding and bruised, I entered the front door. My family happened to be standing there and saw what a mess I was. I felt pretty silly and didn't want to tell them what I had done, but of course I had to offer some explanation for my battered condition. If you can believe it, when I told my tale they laughed at me!

Three weeks later we started out on our family summer vacation. As we began to drive across the desert from Arizona to California, I suggested that we pray for a great vacation and a safe trip. When it was my turn to pray, my son and daughter leaned over the car seat, watching me carefully. After I was done, I had to ask: "Patrick and Shawn, why were you staring at me while I was praying?" They both exclaimed, "We wanted to make sure you didn't close your eyes while you were driving the car!"

You don't have to close your eyes when you pray. In fact, when your eyes are open you can see hospitals, the homeless, schools, accidents, and dozens more scenes where your prayers are needed. All our senses can serve as prayer triggers. When we hear a siren, we can pray for those in need. When we feel hunger pangs, we can pray for the world's starving. And when we are in pain, we can ask God to help everyone who may be suffering.

Other prayer triggers are celebration times. At weddings, we can ask God to reward and refresh all marriages in the world. Birthdays, holidays, promotions, and other pleasant events can be used to trigger prayers of thanks and appreciation.

Praying continually is a way of life. It's like breathing: we don't concentrate on every breath we take. Once we learn to respond with prayer to all that happens around us, we can pray automatically—all of the time.

Today's Prayer

Dear God, use my sense of sight, sound, smell, and touch to trigger prayers. Keep me sensitive to the needs and joys of those around me. Help me get in touch with you, and stay in touch with you every moment of every day. Amen

Growing in Prayer

Write your own list of daily prayer triggers, such as the examples below:

Trigger	*Prayer*
1. Driving by the day care center.	Thanks for the children.
2. Watching the news before bedtime.	Help world leaders to work for justice.
3.	
4.	

Chapter 4

Prayer in Sighs and Screams

———◆———

*That very Spirit intercedes
with sighs too deep for words.*
Romans 8:26

Although words may fail us, God never will!

4

*T*wo old friends were walking through the park one sunny morning. Passing the playground, they watched children of all sizes happily at play. A toddler, running eagerly but unsteadily, tripped and fell headlong onto the ground. His cries rose above the carefree laughter and chatter.

Immediately his mother ran from the bench where she had sat watching him. Gently she picked up her little boy, saw the scrape on his tiny knee, and took him to wash the wound, speaking soothingly to him all the while.

"Isn't that amazing?" one of the elderly gentleman commented.

"What do you mean?" asked the other.

"That child couldn't speak; he could only cry. And yet his mother knew just what he needed and took care of it. You'd think she'd need some words, at least."

"That's not so," said the second. "His mother was watching him. She saw him fall, and she saw the blood on his knee. That's only natural—what any loving parent would do. You've done it yourself with your own children. It would be silly to think that a parent would need a child to talk and explain their hurt before tending to the child's needs."

"I guess you're right," the first gentleman said. He shook his head and smiled. "So why do we seem to have trouble remembering that God knows our needs and sees our hurts, whether we can speak of them or only cry. If an earthly parent is loving enough to watch a child and tend to wounds, how much more is our heavenly Father both eager and able to bring us healing and love?"

◆

Patrick, our three-year-old son, was discovered at the bottom of our friend's swimming pool. My wife Mary jumped into the cold water wearing her nightgown. When she emerged, Mary held in her grasp Patrick's blue, cold, unconscious, lifeless body.

As Mary laid his little body on the cool deck, she immediately placed her lips over Patrick's and blew life-giving air into his lungs. Nothing happened. She tried again and again with no response. Because Mary was in such a state of panic, she had not thought to turn Patrick over to allow the pool water to drain out. Mary just blew harder and harder.

Suddenly Mary looked up into the heavens and screamed, "God, no! You can't let him die!" Once more she blew breath into Patrick's tiny mouth. A little whimper sounded. Mary continued her life-saving measures until the paramedics arrived. Then they took over and stabilized little Patrick enough to transport him by ambulance to the hospital.

After the emergency room doctor finished working with Patrick, he came to the room where Mary and I anxiously waited. "It looks like Patrick is going to be okay," he said. "But we need to keep him here overnight for observation." The next morning as we checked Patrick out of the hospital, we learned that a miracle had indeed taken place. The water that had saturated Patrick's lungs had miraculously disappeared. There was no brain or other physical damage. Mary's screaming prayer had been answered.

A couple at Community Church of Joy who knows what it is to be numbed by tragedy told of a plane crash that occurred when the husband was in the Air Force. One Sunday morning, fifteen men from their base, including their best friend, were killed.

"We came home from church to find an official car waiting outside our neighbor's home. All I could pray was, 'Oh, God!' The entire base was numbed by the shock. It seemed no one was untouched by the tragedy. No prayer could change what had happened, and for days all I and many others could pray was, 'Oh, God!' But that prayer was like a hand to hold on to. And through it God was at work, comforting, sustaining, giving courage, and beginning to heal."

When our heart is crushed or numbed by tragedy or trauma, words are often inadequate to express our thoughts and feelings. Sometimes all we can do is scream or sigh. It's great to know that God hears, understands, and answers those kinds of prayers.

God is in touch with us twenty-four hours a day, seven days a week, throughout our entire life. There is not a moment, awake or asleep, when God is not by our side and on our side. We can be confident that whether we groan or moan, cry or sigh, scream or steam, God hears and answers.

Today's Prayer

Dear God, when Jesus sweat drops of blood, sighed, and cried, you answered his prayers. Thank you for answering my silent prayers as well. Today I can live with hope and courage because you hear me and know me intimately. I love you for caring about me. Amen

Growing in Prayer

Think about a time when your life was out of control. Now imagine yourself gathering that experience up and giving it to God. Write down how you feel.

Chapter 5

Prayer in Desperation

———◆———

Listen to my cry,
for I am in desperate need.
Psalm 142:6 NIV

Despair, from the Latin *desperare*
[*de* "away" + *sperare* "to hope"]
Despair: "away to hope"

Prayer, from the Latin *precarius*
"obtained by entreaty"
Prayer: "a way to hope"

5

"*A* hiker was walking through the forest one day," said the Master, "when she stumbled over a tree root and fell into a deep pit. The sides of the pit were steep and too slick for the hiker to climb out. She had a coil of rope hanging from her belt, so she made a loop in one end and threw the rope up over the edge of the pit. But the rim of the pit was covered with a thick layer of leaves, and there was nothing close by for the loop to catch on. So no matter how many times she threw the rope, it was useless to her."

The Master continued. "Then the hiker heard the crunch of footsteps on the leafy forest floor. She called out for help, and over the edge of the pit a concerned face appeared. It was another hiker. The woman in the pit explained, 'I can't climb out of this slippery hole, but I do have a rope. If I throw it up to you, can you hold the end and help me climb out?'

" 'Sure,' answered the other hiker. 'Throw me the rope. I'll brace my feet on this root. I'm sure I'm strong enough to hold you.' So the trapped hiker threw up the rope. The second hiker caught the rope, braced himself, and holding one end of the rope, threw the looped end down to the hiker. Quickly the first hiker clambered up the slippery wall and over the edge to safety.

"Now what," the Master asked, "rescued the helpless hiker? Was it the rope?"

"No," the disciple replied, "not the rope alone, for by itself the rope couldn't free her from the pit. It wasn't just the rope; it was the one who held it."

"Exactly," stated the Master. "And so it is with prayer. It is not our words—our prayers alone—that rescue us. It is the presence and the strength of God, the one who holds the rope for us."

---◆---

"My husband was laid off the day the Gulf War began," a friend shared with me. "He sent out over a hundred resumes and spent countless days on the phone pursuing interviews. He was offered a job that looked like the answer to our prayers; it was still in the aerospace industry, and the firm was just two miles from our church. We could move and end our long commute every Sunday. It seemed perfect.

"But the job fell through just before he was going to sign the contract. We were stunned. Would God hold out that kind of hope for us, like water to a thirsty child, only to snatch it away? We couldn't understand why it had happened. Six months went by with no job in sight. We had gone through his severance and our savings and by the end of July his unemployment compensation would run out. I understood, for the first time, how easy it could be for an average family to slip into the ranks of the homeless.

"We prayed, believed, cried, and praised, but it seemed God had turned a deaf ear to us. One night in mid-July I woke up, unable to sleep because I was so upset. I went out to the living room and cried out to God, 'I don't understand why you've deserted us.' In the dark silence that followed my cry, slowly a new thought came to me: this isn't about a job, or money. It's about what I believe about God. So I cried out again, 'I don't care that this looks hopeless. I believe you love us, God, and I refuse to believe otherwise.'

"A feeling of joy began to roll over me. Nothing had changed in our circumstances, but something had changed in me. Just a few days later my husband interviewed for another position. The company offered him a job on Friday of that week. It wasn't the position he'd interviewed for, but a better one. He did start at a lower salary than he had in his previous job, so it still hasn't been easy, but now we see that this job may well be the road to another desire we've been praying about for almost twelve years. God heard my prayer, but more importantly, I heard God."

Our prayers in times of desperation are not *our* sirens to get *God's* attention. God knows what is going on before we do. The truth is that we can confidently shout, no matter how desperate we feel, because we already have God's help.

Desperation comes when we believe that we are out of options. But always remember: when we are out of options, God is not! When Jesus was suffering on the cross, he wondered if God had forsaken him. But he still cried out to God.

We never need to hesitate to call out to God, even when we feel most helpless. There is no one more eager and ready to help than our God, the one who loves us most. Even though we can't imagine any way out of a problem, God will show us a way.

Today's Prayer

Dear God, when things are going well, it's easy for me to believe that you are in every situation. Help me to believe, even when I am desperate, that you are with me. Thank you! Amen

Growing in Prayer

List several things—people, relationships, or circumstances—that you have no power to change. Now commit them in prayer to God's love and care.

Chapter 6

Prayer on the Edge of Death

◆

To die is gain.
Philippians 1:21 NIV

Death comes to write the final chapter,
but God adds the final words:
"To be continued."

6

*C*onsider the chemical name for salt: sodium chloride, from sodium and chlorine. Sodium is a poisonous metal, and chlorine is a poisonous gas. Did you ever stop to wonder how two poisonous elements can combine to produce something as beneficial as common salt?

When a sodium atom and a chlorine atom collide, the sodium atom gives up one electron to the chlorine atom. This reaction produces a sodium ion and a chlorine ion, which in turn form crystals of sodium chloride, or salt. By "losing" part of its original nature, the sodium is transformed, if you will, taking on a new nature. What was deadly now melts ice, preserves, brings healing, and seasons food.

Remarkable as it seems, this is not uncommon in the natural world. Consider a cloud. In and of itself, it looks lovely, but when the cloud "loses" itself and condenses into water, it becomes life-giving rain. A candle may also be beautiful in and of itself, but when its wax and wick are melted and burned, it becomes light giving. All of life is a process of transformation.

Is death an ending, or is death a new beginning? For a Christian, death does not have the last word. God promises that the last word belongs to him, and it will be good! This is the reason we can pray with confidence and courage in the face of death. But what do we pray for on the edge of death?

Dad was one of my best friends. Now he was living on the edge of death. Cancer was destroying his body, slowly yet viciously. At first I prayed for healing that would bring him complete recovery. As time passed, however, Dad's dignity and strength suffered severe blows. In my prayers I asked God to let Dad die in peace.

I struggled with this prayer for death. I would really miss my father, but when I watched Dad suffer and deteriorate I was sure this was more than any human being should have to endure.

This struggle is shared by almost everyone who loves someone who is on the edge of death. How does a person pray?

The person dying often prays, more than anything else, that his or her loved ones will be taken care of and that God will give them the gift of heaven. Often the dying person's tears and silence express requests beyond words. God promises to listen to those prayers as well.

Those who pray for a friend or family member find death stirs up extremely strong emotions, and they worry about praying the "wrong prayer." The best way to pray is to be honest with God. Express your dearest thoughts, feelings, and fears. God is the dying person's very best friend. God knows and will do exactly what needs to be done. God knows, because God was there when his one and only son died on the cross. Certainly God will be with each one who belongs to him, through life, on the edge of death, and forever.

The story is told about a little boy walking hand-in-hand with his mother through an art gallery. They stopped to look at a painting depicting the crucifixion of Christ. The scene, showing blood slipping down Christ's face from his forehead pierced by the crown of thorns, was vivid. Suddenly the little boy exclaimed, "God, if you would have been there, this wouldn't have happened." What the boy did not yet know is that God was there when Jesus Christ walked on the edge of death and we can count on the fact that God will also be with us.

We might wish we did not have to face death. We might desire that the cloud remain to give us shade. We might try to preserve the candle so that we can enjoy its beauty. But when the air turns cold and the cloud falls to earth as rain, when the flame burns and melts the candle into light, and when death comes into our own lives, then we can be certain that God's plan for us is transformation. We can also trust that God will be with us in every transforming moment.

When my dad had only hours left to live, he prayed, "I have fought the good fight. I have finished the race. I am now ready to meet the One who loves me most." A short time later he died.

Where does that hope come from, the ability to stare death in the face and know that death is not a punishment? That hope certainly comes from Jesus Christ, who said: "Do not let your hearts be troubled . . . In my Father's house are many rooms . . . I am going there to prepare a place for you . . . I will come back and take you to be with me, that you also may be where I am" (John 14:1-3 NIV).

Today's Prayer

Dear God, thank you that because you conquered death, I can face death knowing that it is a prelude to the victory of eternal life. Thank you for the gift of Jesus, my Savior. Thank you for the assurance that because Jesus lives, I will live also. Amen

Growing in Prayer

Look up and read the prayer Jesus prayed when he was on the edge of death in Matthew 26:36-42.

Chapter 7

Prayer and Family

———◆———

He and all his family
were devout and God-fearing.
Acts 10:2 NIV

Faith is the foundation
and prayer is the mortar
with which we build
a strong and secure life.

7

*T*wo neighbors were painting the picket fence that separated their back yards. "You certainly know your way around a paintbrush," Elizabeth said to Trina.

"I should," replied Trina. "My family had a cabin in the mountains, and I helped oil the siding every summer. Dad taught me to load the brush just right, and of course he showed me how to clean the brushes."

"Did you have to climb a ladder?" Elizabeth asked.

Trina smiled. "Oh, yes," she said. "Dad made sure I learned the whole job. He started by teaching me the most important thing: how to brace the ladder. Our cabin was on a steep, rocky hill, so you couldn't just lean the ladder against the cabin and start climbing!"

Trina smiled as she remembered her lessons. "For two years I watched Dad plant our extension ladder on a wide board, bracing the board so it wouldn't slip. And then one day Dad told me I could do the south side of the cabin."

Elizabeth shuddered. "Weren't you nervous?" she asked.

"I was terrified!" Trina exclaimed. "But Dad helped me brace the ladder the first time, and he watched me go up. And after that it wasn't so bad. I actually got to the point," she admitted, "where I enjoyed oiling the cabin. It gave me time to think . . . and pray!"

Both women laughed. "You know," Trina reflected, "there have been plenty of steep, slippery places in our lives, but prayer has always been there to steady us. I guess you could say," she added, "that the most important thing my dad taught me was how to brace my ladder."

You have probably heard it said that the family that prays together stays together. If you have never prayed for a family member, how do you begin?

I start with a simple "thank you" for each person. As I pray I write notes about each one's pain or sorrow or crushed dreams and about their new, delightful dreams. I ask God what to pray for. Then I am quiet and I listen. After some time of silence, I talk with God about the things that are most pressing.

I have made a promise to my family to pray for them every day, so sometimes they leave me notes or call or write to let me know what they want me to pray for. Often I simply ask them what they want me to pray for.

What if you want to begin praying *with* a family member? It's usually easiest to pray with small children. Every evening a friend of mine prays with her young son, beginning with a simple dialog:

(*Mother*) "Good evening, God."

(*Child*) "Good evening, God."

(*Mother*) "Thank you for this day."

(*Child*) "And thank you, God, for mommy and me and daddy."

"Our prayers are casual and conversational," my friend explains. "We go into the events of the day, thanking God for the good things that happened. I'll say something, then pause to give my son a chance to add his thoughts. Sometimes I pray for our friends' needs, like healing for a friend who has the chicken pox, or help to make a wise decision. I pray for people and places we've heard about on the evening news. Sometimes my son surprises me with the things he picks up. He prays for people in wars or other trouble. We usually end by praying for sweet thoughts and happy dreams, and thanking God for our safety."

The family prays before meals, too, even in public. "If we're at a restaurant and my husband or I forget," my friend explains, "my son is sure to ask, 'Aren't we going to pray?' "

My friend also teaches her son that praying is about more than thanking and asking. "The hardest thing for me to do at first was to confess that I'd been wrong and to pray for forgiveness, especially when my son was the one I wronged. But I think it's important to help my son learn that prayer helps heal broken relationships."

Teaching our children about the gift of prayer is a lifetime treasure. Through the growing years, prayer keeps a family in touch with the heart of God and with each other.

Today's Prayer

Dear God, thank you for family. Help me to remember to bring my needs, and theirs, to you every day. Keep my family close to you and close to one another. Amen

Growing in Prayer

In your mind, form a picture of each person in your family. As you hold each image in your mind, tell God two needs that he or she has. If you have a broken, strained relationship with that family member, thank God for that person. Then ask God what you can do to bring healing to the relationship.

Chapter 8

Prayer
for Safety

---◆---

*For he will hide me in his shelter
in the day of trouble.*
Psalm 27:5

Prayer is our connection to Christ's protection.

8

"You sure are taking a lot of luggage with you just to go on spring break," Noah, a college student, called to his friend Jeff as they passed in the hallway on another trip from their dorm to the parking lot. "Aren't you going to the beach like the rest of us?"

"Yes, but I'm going there to dive," Jeff replied. "That takes a lot more equipment than a bathing suit and a beach towel."

"From the looks of that bag you're carrying, it must!" remarked Noah. "What all do you have in there?"

"Well, this bag has my wet suit, my buoyancy compensator, my mask, my gloves, and my light," said Jeff, mentally going through his checklist. "My friends from the dive shop are bringing the other stuff, like tanks, regulators, and gauges, that I just rent for the dive."

"You really need all that stuff?" Noah inquired as the two walked to Jeff's car.

"Yep! Believe it or not, these are just the essentials. The ocean is fun, but it's a hostile environment," said Jeff. "It's incredibly beautiful, but to experience it safely, a diver has to have the right equipment. When I just go snorkeling in the shallows, all I need are my mask and fins and snorkel. But to dive deeper, I need more. In fact," he added, "I need even more protection than my equipment alone can give."

"What else could you possibly need?" Noah asked, gesturing to the growing pile in the trunk of his friend's car.

"Prayer," said Jeff. "I need it when I'm diving, just like I need it here in school. Prayer doesn't take me out of a hostile environment, but it does help me to live in it more freely."

Jeff smiled. "Prayer sort of works like all my diving gear. For example, prayer helps give me clear vision just like my diving mask. It helps me make the most of my strength like my fins do. Prayer is my life support, just like my air tanks and regulator and gauges. And just like in diving, you always have a partner. In prayer my 'diving partner' is God."

"Wow, *prayer*. All of that equipment in one little word!" Noah pondered for a moment. "Now that I could even fit into my dorm room!"

----------◆----------

Danger is no stranger to anyone. Just look in the news. It's easy to see. Floods, fires, earthquakes, crime, and violence strike hard.

Does God care about my safety? Can God keep me safe? The answer is "Yes!" God promises, "I will keep you safe."

God is even more concerned about my safety than I am. Certain of that, I can relax in the security of the apostle Paul's assurance in Romans 8:38-39 (NIV):

For I am convinced that neither death nor life,
neither angels nor demons, neither the present
nor the future, nor any powers, neither height
nor depth, nor anything else in all creation, will
be able to separate us from the love of God that
is in Christ Jesus our Lord.

Praying for safety is simply asking God to do what God wants to do anyway. Prayer wraps a blanket of safety around us. When we pray, we become more sensitive to danger, which helps us avoid it. And when danger is upon us, prayer can keep us safe in the midst of it. Prayer surrounds us with provision for our physical, emotional, and mental safety.

Colonel Tom Schafer was held hostage in Iran for 444 days. He says that prayer was the reason he was able to survive. Through abusive interrogation, filthy living conditions, and bitterly brutal emotional battles for himself and his comrades, prayer was the only connection to safety.

After many days of captivity in solitary confinement, Tom was placed with some of the other hostages. One of the men had stopped eating and drinking and had attempted suicide numerous times. Tom went over to him and prayed for this broken and battered hostage. Tom started to pray out loud. During his prayer, the man opened his eyes. As Tom prayed the Lord's Prayer, he heard a faint voice praying along with him! Prayer sparked new life in this man; eventually he recovered and returned safely home.

Certainly prayer doesn't always stave off death or war or trouble, but it places us safely in Jesus' care, no matter what the situation or outcome.

Today's Prayer

Loving Lord, keep me safe today, tomorrow, and forever. I am trusting you to do what you promise you will. I love you. Amen

Growing in Prayer

On a slip of paper, write your own prayer for safety. Fold it up and put it in your wallet as a reminder to pray for the safety of yourself and of your loved ones.

Chapter 9

Prayer
for Hope

———◆———

Put your hope in God.
Psalm 42:5 NIV

Hope in circumstance
and your hope will not endure.
Put your hope in God
and your hope will be secure.

9

"Which of you," the Teacher said, "when building a house in the country, would run the plumbing from a seasonal stream into the house? Would you not look to the source of the water—to the water table—and drill a well down to that level where the source of water would not change with the weather or seasons?

"Why, then, look for hope from other people, or circumstances, or situations that can change like the weather? Run the pipe of prayer to God, to the source of hope, and you will find there a sure supply."

Emil Brunner, a 20th century Swiss theologian, said, "What oxygen is to the lungs, hope is to the soul." We all need hope to cope. In fact, when we have hope in the future, we have power to live in the present, too. God wants to give us this hope, even more than we want to ask for it. So God invites us to keep praying for hope for ourselves as well as for others.

When Jesus Christ rose from the dead, hope took on new meaning. The power God demonstrated by raising Jesus from the dead is the same power that gives us reason to hope today. The hope we pray for is not weak or limited. Rather, it is so powerful that it transfigures us. It makes us into new creatures—children of God who need never fear.

I like to tell the story of three-year-old Sara Johnson. Her tiny heart barely quivered for eight straight days. Her mother and father didn't give up the hope of finding a heart for the transplant that could change everything. All their friends joined their prayer for hope.

In another hospital, four-year-old Tara Anderson was about to die from a ruptured artery in her brain that had left her brain dead. Tara's mother and father learned about Sara and lovingly donated Tara's heart to her. Sara received Tara's heart, but five days later the two little girls who had shared a heart now shared heaven together.

The story doesn't end there, though. A short time later, Sara's mother, Paula, found out that she had cancer. Not long after that she also discovered she was pregnant. Even though Paula was advised to abort the child because of the possible effects of the serious cancer treatment she needed, Paula continued in prayer, hoping that she would live to give birth to a healthy child. Nine months later, she gave birth to a healthy baby. On Thanksgiving Day in 1993, at Community Church of Joy, the Andersons and Johnsons reunited in celebration as I baptized that miracle child.

Certainly Sara and Tara can never be replaced, but their legacy is hope. We hoped for life and celebrated God's yes—the answer to our prayer. But hope is not anchored in circumstances. Rather, it is anchored in the character of the God who loves us.

After the deadly earthquake in San Francisco a few years ago, one of our members contacted a brother who lived in Monterey, not far from the quake's epicenter. Though buildings much further from the epicenter were badly damaged, the damage to his home was limited to a few broken dishes. In an earthquake, the most severe damage occurs to structures built on loose, shifting ground. He reassured his sister that he was safe, and would be safe, because Monterey is built on bedrock.

God's goodness does not shift or change; God's love is like bedrock. And that is the hope we have, whether our house is on bedrock or loose soil, whether our circumstances are firm or shaky: God's power and God's love for us stand sure.

Anchor your hope in God. Though the ground around you may be shaken, your hope will endure.

Today's Prayer

Dear God, I am praying right now because I haven't given up hope. I believe in you and I believe that you answer prayers for hope. Please fill me with hope for _____ (*a specific need*). Thank you for your promise that your hope will never disappoint me. Amen

Growing in Prayer

Call a friend or family member today and let the person know that you offered a prayer for him or her, asking God to bring strength through hope.

Chapter 10

Prayer
and My Job

———◆———

Whatever you do,
work at it with all your heart.
Colossians 3:23 NIV

My first job is not what I do for a living.

10

*T*he student leaned over her teacher's shoulder, watching him carefully turn and grind what had once been a shapeless lump of rock into a beautifully faceted stone. "It still amazes me," she said, "how what to an untrained eye appears to be an unimpressive chunk of corundum can become a sparkling ruby. I sometimes wonder if I will ever be able to create a gem as you do."

"I felt the same way looking over my teacher's shoulder," her instructor replied. "It takes many years of experience, as well as a steady hand and an artist's eye, to facet well."

"It amazes me, too, that a proper cut actually adds strength and brilliance to the stone," the student noted.

"Yes, it is amazing" agreed the teacher. "My own instructor taught me that expert gem cutting begins with the ability to see the possibilities and recognize the best cut in each stone. This corundum was formed under enormous heat and pressure. Sometimes the result is a clear crystal whose priceless potential is easily recognized. Sometimes the crystal is flawed, or of less obvious quality. But even then, with a skillful hand and imagination, a gem cutter might still craft something of beauty and value. It's what you bring to the stone, as much as the stone itself, that determines how valuable it will be," concluded the teacher.

"Do you think I will be able to cut gems of such beauty as yours?" asked the student.

"God cares about your work—that you do it well and that you find joy in it. Ask God to give you a steady hand, and to give you imagination to perceive the possibilities," the teacher said. "Couple that with a willingness to learn and your own ability and diligence, and you can learn to bring out the best in any stone."

◆

Nearly half of your life will be spent on the job. Your job is important to you, and it is important to God. Care enough and dare enough to pray about your job. Pray for the right job. Pray for the right compensation. Pray for the right location. Pray for the people you work with.

In 1975 my family and I were driving back to our home in Minnesota from a conference we had participated in on the west coast. While driving through Phoenix, Arizona, my wife and I felt an empowering desire to live and work there someday. When we talked and dreamed about the possibilities, we became even more excited.

Throughout the next three years we continued to pray about our future. As I entered my senior year of seminary I received a call from a church in—guess where—Phoenix, Arizona. My entire family was overjoyed. We thanked God for all of the possibilities that lay ahead of us.

God created every one of us in his image. Crafted within each person are terrific talents and a wonderful personality. Each of us has all the right stuff needed to accomplish everything God imagined when we were created. The secret is to develop our gifts, then match them with a job that maximizes the gifts we have. When this happens, we feel great fulfillment and enjoyment.

The reality is that job satisfaction and success don't come from simply finding the right job. Job satisfaction and success come from being the right employee or employer. Our jobs will never bring us happiness. We are the ones who bring happiness to our jobs.

Ann-Marie frequently complained about how unhappy her job made her. She grew increasingly miserable until she developed a chronic physical illness. When Ann-Marie came to me for counsel, she was very discouraged. I dared to ask her, "Since your job isn't giving you any happiness, are willing to try bringing happiness to your job?" The light went on!

What we bring to our job has a powerful effect on what we get out of our job. This discovery helped Ann-Marie transform her expectations. She was the key to her happiness—not her job.

How do you pray, then, for yourself or someone else who is in a job fraught with frustration? Friends of ours know someone in that position. A highly educated and highly skilled professional, he was nevertheless out of work for two years. Before he found a permanent position, he supported his family by digging foundations. The job he finally found has been filled with struggles and obstacles.

"After two years of unemployment, how can he think of quitting?" our friends commented. "We do pray that he will find a better job, but we've started praying until that job comes, God will show him some way to find peace of mind and satisfaction in the work he does."

Prayer shapes our attitudes, our spirit, and our heart, as well as our talents. Inviting God to take charge of everything we are, have, and hope to be, is the key to job success and satisfaction.

Today's Prayer

Dear God, thank you for letting me know that my job is important to you. I am confident that you will continually help me discover the right job, in the right place, for the right compensation, with the right people. I ask you to help me become an effective and thankful worker. Amen

Growing in Prayer

Write a thank-you note today to the person you work with whom you most appreciate.

Chapter 11

Prayer Habits

---◆---

Pray without ceasing.
1 Thessalonians 5:17

Your prayer life will become uncommonly rich
when prayer becomes a common occurrence.

11

*C*onsider the force that builds stone formations within a cave. Water sinks down through layers of organic matter in the soil, becoming carbonic acid, carbon dioxide dissolved in water. This acid dissolves limestone below the soil, carrying minerals with it.

If the acid seeps into a cave that has an opening to the outside, enabling air to enter the cave, the carbon dioxide bubbles out of the acid the same way the fizz escapes from a bottle of soda, and the water becomes less acidic. No longer able to dissolve limestone, the water droplet also can no longer carry its already-dissolved limestone. When the droplet evaporates, it leaves behind a minute deposit of calcium carbonate. Over time the calcium carbonate builds up into lovely forms: stalactites, stalagmites, draperies, columns, curving helictites.

Is it the occasional force of mighty water that builds these lovely forms? No, it is water droplets, working one drop at a time. Each drop leaves its mark behind. Each drop contributes to a growing, singularly lovely form.

In the same way, a life of prayer is built. Each prayer changes the person who prays, somehow, enriching them and helping them to grow. Your life can be changed, shaped into a form uniquely beautiful as you pray steadily, drop by drop, one prayer at a time.

———◆———

Prayer is a good habit. We all have many good habits. On the other hand, we all have at least a few bad habits. How can we develop good habits like prayer, and get rid of bad habits? A simple answer is to pray for God to develop good habits in our lives and destroy the bad habits.

Let's do that right now:
Dear God, please help me develop good habits
in my life today, and please help me let go of
the bad habits. Give me the wisdom to know the
difference. Amen.
Habits begin with our thoughts, not our feelings. Our
thoughts produce our actions. Our repeated actions develop our habits. If we want good habits then we must begin
with good thoughts. Life is where my actions begin. I start
every day with this prayer of St. Augustine:
Take my mind and think through it.
Take my knowledge and set it on fire.
Take my heart and flood it with your love.
Love the world through me. Amen.
St. Augustine's prayer shapes my thoughts, which
flow into action, producing a habit. (Loving the world is a
tremendous habit!)
Another helpful prayer habit is prayer journaling.
Prayer has not always been one of my good habits. I let
the pressures and distractions in my life displace prayer.
When I let this happen I felt like my emotional and spiritual fuel tank was on empty. About three years ago I
bought a little notebook and began writing down names
of people I wanted to pray for, problems I wanted to
solve, needs I wanted met, things for which I wanted to
praise God, discoveries I wanted to make, and dreams I
wanted fulfilled.
I began writing for ten minutes or so, then twenty
minutes, then longer. It amazed me to see how God answered the prayers I recorded in my journal. Keeping a
prayer record reinforced the good habit of prayer.
Prayer journaling doesn't have to be limited to keeping a notebook, however. One man I know goes to work a
few minutes early each day to pray as he puts his journal
entries on his computer. Others have told me that they
keep a journal on a cassette tape recorder.
Another practical idea is to keep a small prayer datebook in your purse or briefcase. When a concern comes

to your mind, or when someone asks you to pray for them, you can record the concern or request in your datebook as a reminder both to pray and to look for the answer.

You can begin to develop your own prayer habits today. Be creative about developing your habits. Go for prayer walks, or prayer hikes, or prayer trips, or try prayer journaling, or prayer singing, or prayer reading, or _____. You fill in the blank!

Today's Prayer

Dear God, help me to think prayer thoughts, take prayer actions, and turn these thoughts and actions into prayer habits. Amen

Growing in Prayer

Identify one prayer habit you want to develop today. Write it down here.

_____

Now write down the first two steps you plan to take to grow into that habit.

1. _____

2. _____

Now begin!

Chapter 12

Prayer in the Midst of Failure

For whenever I am weak, then I am strong.
2 Corinthians 12:10

Failure often looks like the absence of success,
but failure can become the first step
toward true success.

12

"And this is a picture of our softball team," Peggy said, holding out a snapshot. "Joining the team was one of the best things I've done since I retired."

"From the picture, it looks like you all feel that way," commented Julie.

"We're all smiles here," Peggy acknowledged, "and strangely enough, this shot was taken just after a game we lost badly. But you know, that's not what I see when I look at this picture," Peggy continued. "When I got these photos back, I wanted to make some copies of this picture for the team. Looking through the negatives, it became clear that the development process takes a dim, murky-looking negative and turns it into a beautiful positive photo, with the colors true and the lights and darks in their proper balance."

"I know what you mean," said Julie. "Even though it's hard to recognize a good looking photo from its negative, the processing makes it turn out right."

"Yes," laughed Peggy. "it dawned on me that my failures are a lot like a photo negative. Too often I leave them at that stage—a negative. But when I take them to God in prayer, God helps me process that failure, and use it to create something positive and beautiful."

◆

Abraham Lincoln, Thomas Edison, Sister Kenny, Corrie ten Boom, and numerous others were no strangers to failure. These creative geniuses welcomed failure because it helped them discover something that didn't work, then took them one step closer to discovering a way that did work. Failure can help us turn to God in prayer because praying about failure helps us put it into proper perspective.

Within a year after I became the pastor of Community Church of Joy, half of the members had left. There were secret meetings in homes where church leaders plotted to get rid of me. During one 4½-hour public meeting I was verbally attacked and I went home literally shivering from flu-like chills.

Not long after that experience I received a phone call that the church kitchen was on fire. I rushed to my car to go meet the fire fighters, but I couldn't move. I was paralyzed with the feeling of failure. With tears streaming down my cheeks I cried out to God, "Help me!"

In the midst of this new crisis, I sensed God's unconditional love wrap around me. My feelings of failure had pressed me right up against God's heart. There I felt more peaceful and confident than I had in months. When I became the weakest, God became the strongest. That was a turning point for me and the church in our ministry.

When failure comes, we often want to fight it or deny it or blame it on people and circumstances. We see failure as something to run from instead of something to learn from. But through prayer we can develop the courage to fail, believing that God can transform our failure into a force that moves us forward, no matter what happens.

Cliff and Paula took out a second mortgage on their home to help finance their dream of owning their own business. Ten months after their store opened, Paula says, they were trying to sell as much of their inventory as possible in the front of their store while carpenters tore down the shelves in the back of the store to begin remodeling for the new owners. Paula and Cliff faced not only the emotional blow of seeing their dream literally coming down around them, but also the potentially disastrous debt from their venture. "Strangely enough, the whole time I had such a peace about the situation," Paula notes. "And we found so much strength from the people who stuck by us."

Times were rough for quite a while, but Paula says, "That taught us that we had to trust the Lord. And I have never felt ashamed of the fact that we opened and closed in ten months."

Cliff and Paula gladly tell their story to anyone who will listen. "Knowing the end result—our own growth, and finding such beautiful people to support us—I'd go through it all again," Paula joyfully declares.

Today's Prayer

Dear God, help me to handle my failure successfully by placing it into your hands. Thank you for being with me during the tough times. Amen

Growing in Prayer

Write down your biggest failure on a piece of paper. If you can find two pieces of wood, place them in the shape of a cross. (If you cannot, follow this process in your imagination.) With a hammer and a nail, put the nail through the piece of paper and hammer it to the cross. Say out loud, "Thank you, Jesus, that I can place my failure in your hands. I ask you to transform my failure into a new beginning."

Chapter 13

Prayer and Suffering

———————◆———————

Suffering produces perseverance;
perseverance, character; and character,
hope. And hope does not disappoint us.
Romans 5:3-5 NIV

Jesus knows your suffering firsthand.
Ask for his hand to help you stand.

13

"*I*'m glad you made it!" a hiker called down from the hilltop to a group of hikers who had just arrived, flushed and tired, at a campsite.

"We wouldn't have," panted the leader of the new arrivals, "if it hadn't been for you and the trail markers you left across that field of boulders."

"And we might have missed the spot where the trail led off from the creek bank if you hadn't tied that piece of red cloth to the bush," one women added.

"Well, I've struggled to find a trail a time or two myself," the first hiker confessed, coming down from the hill to join the group, "and I know how it feels to want to give up. So I was glad you asked for my help earlier today. In fact, I was looking for you from the hilltop."

"It helps to know there's a trail to follow," said the group's leader, "but it's better still to know someone who knows the way firsthand, and cares that you make it through."

———————◆———————

Suffering certainly isn't any fun. It can, however, have significant results. This prayer explains it best:

> I prayed for strength, that I could be strong;
> I was made weak, that I could be more tender.
> I prayed for health, that I could accomplish
>   greatness;
> I was given sickness, that I could do better
>   things.
> I prayed for wealth, so that I could be satisfied;
> I was made poor, so that I could have wisdom.

I prayed for power, so that I could rule the
    world;
I was given brokenness, so that I would depend
    on God.
I prayed for many things, so that I could enjoy
    life;
I was given "new life," so that I could enjoy
    many things.
I didn't get what I prayed for, but I got every-
    thing I longed for.
("A Creed for Those Who Have Suffered," *Chick-
    en Soup for the Soul*, p. 268.)

It has been said that the presence of evil in the world
and the suffering that comes from it is the single greatest
challenge to the Christian faith. People have tried for centuries, without success, to understand *why* people suffer.
In the end, we cannot understand, but we can turn to God
who gave his Son Jesus to suffer and die, and to rise
again from the grave. That is why prayer and suffering belong together. Prayer puts us in touch with the one who
knows everything about suffering.

When we suffer, or when we watch children or members of our family or a friend suffer, we might feel dis-
gusted or even angry with God. Praying in the face of suffering helps us deal with our feelings so that we do not
think of God as an enemy at the very time we need God's
friendship most. Even if we understandably cannot see
any *good* in the suffering, prayer can help us see *God!*

When we suffer, we not only need God. We need people to cry with and sigh with. Often the ones we can turn
to are those who have themselves suffered most. They often seem the most understanding and approachable. A
woman in our congregation says she can see some good
now that came from a seven-year period of longing and
repeated unsuccessful efforts to conceive a child. "After
what we went through," she explains, "even though our
story has a happy ending, now when I listen to someone

who is childless, I can honestly say 'I can imagine how you might feel,' because I have been there."

Just as this woman is able to comfort others because she suffered, so, the Bible tells us, God brings comfort to us:

Praise be to the God and Father of our Lord Jesus Christ, the Father of compassion and the God of all comfort, who comforts us in all our troubles, so that we can comfort those in any trouble with the comfort we ourselves have received from God. For just as the sufferings of Christ flow over into our lives, so also through Christ our comfort overflows. (2 Corinthians 1:3-5 NIV)

No one knows more about comforting those who suffer than God. You can call on God anytime to help you walk through the corridors of suffering.

Today's Prayer

Dear God, it is hard to see through the suffering today. Thank you for going before us and for overcoming even the power of death so that we might be assured of your peace. Amen

Growing in Prayer

List your greatest past and present sufferings.

_____

_____

_____

_____

_____

_____

Place one hand palm down over your list. Then as you tell God about each of these, imagine God's hand upon yours. Thank God for being there with you. This week look for someone who is hurting whose hand you can hold.

Chapter 14

Prayer
When Making Decisions

---

*Multitudes, multitudes,
in the valley of decision.*
Joel 3:14

The best choice we can make
is to make God the first part of every choice.

14

"*A* nearsighted man went for a walk one day," the Master began. "He took a compass and map, food and water, and a first-aid kit, and he wore sturdy hiking boots and a hat and carried a walking stick. At the last minute, though, he decided he wouldn't need his glasses. 'I see well enough to get along without my glasses,' he thought to himself. 'My walking stick will be enough. I can use it to clear a path, judge the depth of a stream or the height of a step, and fend off any small, nasty creatures I might meet.'

"So the man set off," continued the Master. But two hours later, he limped, bruised and disheveled, past his neighbor's yard. 'Whatever happened to you?' asked his neighbor, rushing to help the man to his door.

" 'Well, I prepared as well as I could for a pleasant hike,' the man replied, 'but lying on the other side of the log I stepped over was a sleeping porcupine. The leafy glen I walked through was poison oak. And the rock I stood on to jump across a bubbling creek was covered with slippery moss. I just didn't see those . . . details.'

" 'Did you lose your glasses when you fell?' inquired the neighbor.

" 'No, I didn't wear them. I didn't think I'd need them,' the man sheepishly answered."

The Master paused. "Where did the man make his mistake?"

"When he decided not to take his glasses," the disciple said. "His glasses should have been his first choice."

"And going to God in prayer should be our first choice," said the Master. "God's wisdom gives us the 'lens' we need to see the way more clearly than we can see if we rely only on ourselves."

———————◆———————

Making important decisions can be difficult, but we do not need to struggle alone. Through prayer we can invite God to give us wisdom and guidance. In fact, the best way to make the best decisions is to pray about every decision.

The Bible tells the story of King Solomon who asked God for the gift of wisdom. God granted Solomon's request, and Solomon was known throughout the world for his wisdom.

A well-known story illustrates Solomon's incredible wisdom. Two women each claimed to be the mother of a particular child. Obviously, one woman was lying, but to which woman did the baby belong? They asked King Solomon to decide. The king called for a sword so he could cut the infant in half. Then each woman could have half the child. The infant's real mother protested, crying out, "No, let the other woman have the baby. Let him live!"

"Cut the child in half," insisted the other woman.

King Solomon gave the baby to the woman who wanted the child to live. Her willingness to give up the child so he could live demonstrated that she truly loved the child and was clearly the baby's mother.

When we pray about a decision, we open ourselves to God's guidance. God created us, deeply cares what happens to us, and wants the best for us. When we take our decisions to God in prayer, God clarifies our thoughts, opens new options to us, or shows us things we might have overlooked.

One young man prayed about which of two prestigious universities he should attend. Both schools had accepted him but offered little financial aid. While he was still undecided, another school contacted him and offered him a full scholarship. He looked into this new possibility and found that the school offered him courses, mentors, and opportunities he never would have found at either of the other schools. He accepted the scholarship and felt certain that through prayer, God helped him make the best choice.

God promises to be with us, not just when we are making decisions but when we then live with our decisions as well.

Michelle was a young member of our congregation. She was on a life support system. Doctors had determined that nothing more could be done for her. It was time to disconnect the system and let Michelle die naturally. As I met with Michelle's family, we held one another close, and we prayed that the decision to disconnect life support was the best possible decision. That prayer not only helped the family make the decision, but also provided them with God's comfort after the life support was disconnected.

The most important decision we can ever make is to invite God to be a part of every decision we make. With God, we can see more clearly than we ever could alone.

Today's Prayer

Dear God, I want to make the best decisions I can possibly make today. Please help me consider all the facts, forces, and faces. Then give me the courage and confidence to decide. Thank you. I know I can always count on you. Amen

Growing in Prayer

Develop a Decision Diary. First, write down the decision to be made. Next, write a simple prayer asking for God's direct involvement. Finally, record the results of your decision.

Chapter 15

Prayer for Friends

———◆———

I have called you friends.
John 15:15

Through prayer
God can bring and build friendship.

15

*M*arja and Kim went to a folk art festival. Together they watched a weaver at his loom, expertly passing the shuttle back and forth to create an emerging design.

"I'm amazed how you can get endlessly different designs from just a few colors," Marja remarked to the weaver. "And this piece you're weaving now—you've just used two colors, but it's beautiful."

"It's a matter of creating a pattern through the interaction of the warp and the weft yarns," the weaver explained. "Most people don't realize how important the warp is to the design of a piece."

"I know that the warp underlies it all," commented Kim, "and that different patterns are created by going under and over the warp threads in different ways, but what happens if you ignore the warp threads?"

"It's all right to do that over a few warp threads for effect," the weaver replied, "but the weaving would be unanchored if you left out the warp threads for long."

"That's the way it is with God, too," Marja said as the two women walked toward another exhibit. "God is an underlying part of all parts of my life: my job, my family, our friendship."

"You know, you're right. I can look back over all the friends who have touched my life," Kim said thoughtfully, "and see all the colors God has woven through my life. Through the times we've been together, the times we've been apart, the times the weave has been less than smooth, I've always felt that our relationship is special because God is part of it."

"Yes, God has made something extraordinary out of our friendship," said Marja as she clasped Kim's hand.

◆

How are you fixed for friends today? If you have friends, ask God to help you improve your friendships. For many today, life seems so hectic that we hardly have time for the friends we've already made. Every day I pray for my friends. Through prayer I stay in touch, even though we don't necessarily visit one another often. Because I pray for my friends regularly, when we do get together, we are able to pick up where we left off the last time we were together.

If you need a friend, ask God to help you *be* a friend. Being a friend is the best way to have friends. I know a couple that, in the first eighteen months of their marriage, made a series of far-away moves from the places where they grew up. In each new place, one of the first things they did was find a church and ask how they could help the congregation. "We had friends and felt at home from that day on," they said. The key here is that to find friendship, look for a need you can fill. If you are lonely today, ask God to lead you to someone you can serve.

Friendship connections and networks are the most powerful in the world. God knows how important they are. Through them we receive support and encouragement, as well as opportunities to grow. Friendship's force is unstoppable. God created us to live as friends. And God can help us maintain the bonds of friendship.

God can even create friendships beyond the boundaries of distance and time. A member of Community Church of Joy began praying for the Soviet Union and Christians in the USSR fifteen years ago after hearing a missionary speak about the great needs there. Over the years she kept praying.

In the summer of 1992 her oldest son was part of Community Church of Joy's youth evangelism team to St. Petersburg and Moscow. "That gave me a greater sense of intimacy in my prayers for Russian Christians. I knew there was someone specific I was praying for, but I still had no idea who it was," she said.

"Community Church of Joy was providing financial assistance to help four young Russian women attend college in Minnesota," she continued. "The missions office asked us to invite one of the women into our home during Christmas vacation. One day in the midst of the whirl of caroling, parties, and sightseeing, I sat talking on the couch with our guest, Lena. We had met less than two weeks before, but we felt such closeness. She told me about how she became a Christian and about her prayers for her non-Christian family. Slowly something began to dawn on me: I had been praying for this young woman, not knowing who she was, since she was five years old, and here she sat beside me now, my new 'old' friend."

We all need friends. Friendship is one of God's greatest gifts. God offers us his friendship and gives us the gift of friendship with other people. In fact, prayer for friends is a prayer God can't wait to answer. It gives God unbelievable pleasure to fill our life with friends, to show us how to be a true friend, and to be our friend. Be sure not to miss this joy today as you pray for friends you already have, and for new friends.

Today's Prayer

Dear God, thank you that you are my friend. Your friendship makes it possible for me to be to others the friend you have been to me. Please show me how to be a better friend, and show me new people who need me to be a friend. Amen

Growing in Prayer

Make a list of friends and acquaintances. Call or write and ask them if they have a need you could give to God in prayer. Over the course of a few weeks, regularly focus on each friend in prayer.

Chapter 16

Prayer and Stress

———◆———

*Come to me, all you that are weary
and are carrying heavy burdens,
and I will give you rest.*
Matthew 11:28

Through prayer God transforms **stress** into rest.

16

"Which of you," said the Teacher, "when riding a ten-speed up a steep hill, would keep pedaling in the highest gear? Would you not move to a lower gear to help you up the hill when your effort alone could not keep you going?

"So it is with prayer. When stress saps our strength and the situation demands more than we feel we have left to give, we can through prayer shift the burden to God, who is equal to every challenge. With God's help, we can meet the hills in life and keep going."

◆

What should you do when your neck is tense and your shoulders are tight and your head aches from stress? Answer: Pray!

Prayer is the best way to handle stress. Prayer helps us relax by taking our focus off whatever is causing the stress and putting our focus on God. God is the best "stress buster" in the world.

When pressure causes us to feel pressed down, powerless, inadequate, we feel "stressed out."

But when we pray, God causes up to be

lifted up,
*"Humble yourselves before the Lord,
and he will lift you up" (James 4:10 NIV)*

strengthened,
*"He gives power to the faint, and strengthens the
powerless. . . . Those who wait for the Lord shall renew
their strength" (Isaiah 40:29, 31a)*

enabled and empowered.

". . . but he said to me,
'My grace is sufficient for you,
for power is made perfect in weakness.'
So, I will boast all the more gladly of my weaknesses,
so that the power of Christ may dwell in me"
(2 Corinthians 12:9b).

Jesus was under such stress over the crucifixion he was about to endure that he actually sweat like drops of blood. Do you know what he did then? He prayer to God. God was able to handle Jesus' stress, and God can handle yours as well.

Prayer helps us find relaxation and renewal. Many medical stress reduction centers teach the importance of prayer. A surgeon told me that she holds her hands in the air for a quick prayer to help her completely relax before every critical surgical move. Business leaders who are negotiating stressful deals often silently pray for calmness and inner peace, which allows them to proceed at peak performance.

Athletes pray before games for relief from stressful pregame jitters. At every wedding I perform, I privately pray for all the stress-producing nervousness to be taken away. When I give a presentation to a group, I pray for the calm confidence to relax enough to make the best presentation I can possibly make.

Stress causes us to choke. It can literally give us the feeling that hands are around our throat. Through prayer we can break free of the chokehold of stress. Let's pray right now that God will loosen the noose of stress.

Today's Prayer

Dear God, I give you all my stress today. Only you
know how to relieve it all. Help me relax and enjoy
every person and purpose I encounter. Thank you for
the peace you fill me with. Amen

Growing in Prayer

On a sheet of paper, jot down your greatest source of
stress. Crumple the paper up and squeeze it as hard
as you can. Then slowly relax your hand to symbol-
ize your letting go of the stress and releasing it into
God's hands through prayer.

Chapter 17

Prayer and Exercise

———◆———

Everyone who competes in the games goes into strict training. They do it to get a crown that will not last; but we do it to get a crown that will last forever.
1 Corinthians 9:25 NIV

For health, for peace, for strength,
exercise your prayer life, as well as your body.

17

"*T*o exercise your body without exercising your prayer life is to miss a great blessing," the Master told the disciple.

"Think of the dam in the hills above us," directed the Master. "Water can be released through the spillway at the top of the dam, and it flows down to bring life to the valley here below. But that would use only part of the potential of the water. When water is released through the penstock at the bottom of the dam, it flows through a turbine in the powerhouse, then out through the tailrace to the valley below. The same water both produces power for, and gives life to, the valley.

"Physical exercise is like water through a spillway," said the Master. "It brings vitality to your life. But exercise coupled with prayer is like water through a penstock, channeling within you the blessings of both life and power. To strengthen your spirit and mind as you strengthen your body," the Master continued, "is to receive a double reward."

———————◆———————

Prayer and exercise are great companions. During a routine of weight-lifting, aerobics, jogging, walking, bicycling, swimming, or any other form of exercise, we are strengthening our bodies. Why not develop an exercise program for our whole self? Prayer is an excellent exercise workout for our inner being.

When the heart rate is raised and we start to sweat, that's a great time to pray about both problems as well as possibilities. Our minds are clearer and we can listen to the important messages God is eager to communicate with us. It will amaze you how imaginative and creative you can become during a prayer and exercise workout.

My son Patrick and I frequently jog together. We enjoy what we refer to as "popcorn prayer." Whatever pops into our minds, we pray out loud about it. This has deepened our relationship with God and with each other. Our prayer teams at church take prayer hikes and prayer bicycle trips, and they have their own prayer aerobics classes. Those who participate talk enthusiastically about how prayer and exercise compliment each other.

I started to combine prayer and exercise over sixteen years ago. Adding the dimension of prayer to exercise made my exercise time more meaningful and enjoyable. Some people enjoy their prayer and exercise time alone. Others prefer to have a partner. However you want to develop your time, you can be confident that prayer and exercise makes a winning combination.

Our church has many athletic teams: basketball, softball, volleyball, and so on. We have integrated prayer as part of the sporting activity. Many of the participants have remarked how valuable prayer has been in building greater friendship and teamwork. They have learned that prayer isn't something that should be stuffed away in some religious building. Rather, prayer is an important part of everything we do.

Today's Prayer

Dear God, thank you for making prayer so practical and available. Help me make the most out of prayer and exercise. Build in me the desire to stay in shape, both physically and spiritually. Amen

Growing in Prayer

To get started, include prayer during your next exercise experience. If you are not exercising, consider a prayer walk or hike. It will be an invigorating adventure.

Chapter 18

Prayer and Mealtime

———◆———

Give us this day our daily bread.
Matthew 6:11

Gratitude nourishes the heart
as food nourishes the body.

18

"Which of you," the Teacher said, "if you found a wonderful gift at your doorstep, would be so unimpressed that you would discard it without reading any letter or card or shipping label that told you the name of the sender? Would you not be eager to know who sent the gift? And when you looked at or used the gift, would you not be pleasantly reminded of the love that sent it? And would you not be happy to send a thank-you acknowledging your receipt of the gift and your joy in the thoughtfulness of the giver, particularly if you found that the giver was someone who loved you?

"In the same way then, whenever you eat, think of God, the giver of your food. Let your prayers when you eat be a happy note of thanks to the one who truly loves you. Then you will receive not only your food, but also the added gift of a grateful heart."

———◆———

Do you pray before you eat? As a young child, I was encouraged to pray and thank God for my food. Food is a precious gift from God. Without food, we could not live. We should never take food for granted.

The Bible tells us that Jesus prayed before meals. Praying before meals honors the provider, the producer, and the preparer. Thanking God for food gives God great pleasure. Praying before meals also gives God a chance to let us know how we can be a part of helping to feed others.

A friend recounted the story of an unusual shopping trip. She was walking toward the entrance to a supermarket when a scruffy, disheveled looking man approached her. He told her he was hungry and without money. Rather than give him money, she told him she was doing her own grocery shopping and would be happy to buy him some food, too. "I didn't know if he truly wanted food, or if he only wanted money," she said, "but I prayed, 'God, if he is hungry, then bless him through this food. And if he is only looking for money, then touch him anyway through this food.' "

She did her own shopping, and she bought him a loaf of bread, some cheese and meat, some fruit, and some juice. The she had the checker put his things in a separate bag. "When I left the store, the man was still there. I handed him the bag, and said, 'God loves you, and he cares that you are fed.' The man took the bag and with tears in his eyes he hugged me and said, 'God bless you, too.' Then he walked away. As I turned to take the cart of groceries to my car, the store manager rushed out and asked if I was okay. He saw the man hug me and was afraid I'd been assaulted. I assured him I was fine, thinking how humiliated I would feel if people suspected my every action just because I looked poor or dirty."

"I was so thankful that we had food," my friend added. "And several years later, when we had very little income for many months, I was grateful God stretched our resources so that we still could buy food for our family. We really mean it when we say thanks over our food."

Praying regularly before mealtime is a great habit. When our children were young we simply prayed, "Thank you, Jesus, for the food." As they grew older we prayed, "Come, Lord Jesus, be our guest, and let these gifts to us be blessed. Amen." We also prayed, "God is great. God is good. Now we thank him for our food. By his hand we all are fed. Give us, God, our daily bread. Amen."

From time to time, we would get a little more creative about our mealtime prayer. If it was a special occasion, like a birthday, we would pray that God would give many more happy years. We would pray for much success for a graduation celebration, or uncontainable joy for a Christmas celebration. Prayer can make any meal a magnificent time of day, and no doubt God enjoys being a part of our celebration of gratitude for food.

It has been said that not only do we appreciate food more after we pray, we even digest food better! And certainly we honor through our prayer the creator of everything we eat.

Take time to pray at mealtime. Wherever you are, people around you—watching, listening, or praying with you—will be encouraged and enriched through your prayers. Most importantly, God will be complimented!

Today's Prayer

Dear God, remind me to pray for food. I want always to be thankful for both the gift and the giver of the food I eat. Thank you for being my provider. I love you. Amen

Growing in Prayer

Create a new mealtime prayer.

Chapter 19

Prayer and Relationships

———◆———

The greatest of these is love.
1 Corinthians 13:13b

I = PRT
Formula for calculating interest:
Interest = **P**rincipal x **R**ate x **T**ime

Formula for calculating intimacy:
Intimacy = **P**ray for your **R**elationship **T**oday

19

*B*rian held a cleaning rag in his hand as he opened the door for Sandra to come in.

"What are you up to today?" Sandra asked.

"I'm oiling a couple of pieces of furniture," Brian replied. "I have some things that have been in my family for a long time, and I oil the wood to keep it from cracking and drying out."

"These must be important pieces," Sandra said, "for you to put so much effort into them."

"Yes," Brian acknowledged, "they mean a lot to me. I hope to enjoy them for a good many years, and then I want to pass them on to my children. It's really a privilege for me to care for them."

"There is an oil we can use to take care of our relationships, too" said Sandra.

"You're always thinking," laughed Brian. "What is this oil?"

"It's the oil of prayer," Sandra explained. "The oil of prayer sinks in to heal wounds and prevent any cracks from getting deeper. And the oil of prayer enhances and protects the beauty of a relationship, so we can share it with others."

Sandra stopped, a bit surprised with herself. She laughed. "Well, I really didn't come over here to wax poetic about oil and prayer! I just came over to see if you would like me to pray with you about that concern you shared with me yesterday."

"Sure," answered Brian, smiling. "And then I'll find you an extra cloth!"

Prayer produces intimacy. One of the first things I do every morning is pray for my relationships with my family and friends. I ask God to make me the best husband, friend, lover, and encourager I can possibly be.

My wife and I often pray together, and we have found that prayer helps us grow closer to God and one another. Sometimes we pray about things that probably seem pretty ordinary. We turn to prayer when we face things that are unclear or scary. And we often pray for each other and for our relationship.

Here is my "Top Ten" list of things I pray will be part of my relationships:

1. Unconditional love
2. Regular compliments
3. Forgiveness
4. Trust
5. A positive attitude
6. Commitment
7. Respect
8. Joy
9. Compassion
10. Prayer

We can think of prayer as the key to the whole list. Praying *together* with a friend or spouse can be an especially powerful experience. What deeper joy can there be than to hear one who cares about you lifting you in prayer to the God who loves you most?

But where do you begin if you have never prayed with someone else? Holding hands at mealtime can make it easier to begin holding hands when you pray at other times. Holding hands is helpful for most any prayer time. A gentle touch can help two people feel more connected and comfortable when they pray. A simple squeeze of the hand can indicate that one partner is ready for the other to speak or ready to close the prayer.

Listen with a sensitive heart to the words your partner prays and to the movement of the Spirit within you.

Try not to anticipate what you think your partner ought to be praying for. Try to focus on your partner's prayer, rather than on what you want to pray about next.

If you are not used to praying out loud, you might want to pray silently with a prayer partner at first. When you are ready to pray out loud, you probably will find you are more comfortable with a brief, simple, fairly conversational prayer. Don't rush to fill any pause or silence with words. And don't try to create a long, flowery prayer that doesn't communicate real thoughts or needs.

Invite God now to enter into you and all your relationships to help you make them more meaningful and magnificent.

Today's Prayer

Dear God, my relationships belong to you. Help me love unconditionally, forgive, trust, look for the best in, and respect _____ (*name*). I commit myself to growing in my relationship with _____ (*name*). Amen

Growing in Prayer

1. Make a promise with a spouse, child, friend, co-worker, or neighbor to pray for each other daily.
2. Write a note and let someone know you are praying for him or her today.
3. Hold hands with your spouse, another family member, or a friend, and pray for one another.
4. Put a list of the needs of your family members or friends someplace where you'll see it regularly to remind you to pray for them.

Chapter 20

Prayer and Crisis

———◆———

In my distress I called upon the Lord.
2 Samuel 22:7

Crisis disables people.
Prayer enables people.

20

*T*he lifeguards looked around them at the group of children seated on the pool's deck. "Who remembers rule number one? What is the first thing you do if someone falls into the pool?"

"Yell for help!" the young voices chorused.

"That's one rule I have to keep reminding myself to follow," Venita remarked to Renee as they watched their children's swimming lesson.

"Oh? Did you have an accident in your pool?" Renee asked with concern.

"No, no, nothing like that," Venita hurried to explain. "I just mean I wish I could remember to ask for help more readily. Last week, for instance," she continued, "a pipe under the sink sprang a major leak. I panicked at first, and by the time I finally thought to turn off the water supply to the house, I had everybody else in a tizzy, too. I finally calmed down after I called the plumber and I knew help was on the way."

Venita went on. "Later it dawned on me that if I had thought to call for help right away I probably could have saved myself from that panic."

Renee nodded. "I've had trouble myself remembering to go to God for help . . . remembering to pray. But you know what's helping me? I'm trying to make prayer a continual part of my day. That way, when a crisis does occur, it's natural for me to ask God for help first. Then, as you said, I can calm down and trust that help is on the way."

The voices of the children rose again: "Yell for help!" Venita laughed. "I know what will help us both. This week you call me every morning and ask me, 'What's rule number one?' "

◆

Don't panic. Pray! My ten-year-old son and I were playing catch with a football. I threw a long high pass that came down on the tip of Patrick's thumb and dislocated it. He screamed, "Help me, Daddy! Help me!" We rushed my son to the emergency room and got things taken care of. Before too many days he had completely recovered from the crisis.

Patrick did what all of us should do in the midst of crisis: cry out for help. The fact is, there is no one better able to handle a crisis than God. Prayer calls forth all the powers of God to help us through.

A powerful example of this took place in Susi Feldman's life. This 14-year-old got lost during a school field trip. When Susi was rescued after two days in the woods, her rescuers found her praying. She was slightly dehydrated but otherwise in good condition. Her constant prayer provided guidance to the rescue team and encouragement to Susi herself.

In the midst of crisis, praying is the most significant thing we can do. It guides our actions, organizes our thoughts, and channels our emotions in the best possible way.

On August 1, 1943, Walter T. Stewart and his crew set out in their B-24, designated "Utah Man," to bomb Hitler's oil refineries in Romania. Of the nearly 200 bombers that took off for that mission, only a handful returned. Stewart's plane was so badly damaged from anti-aircraft fire that it couldn't possibly keep up with the other surviving bombers to make the trip back to their base in North Africa. To avoid enemy fire, Stewart and his crew were forced to fly so low that Utah Man literally brushed the treetops.

With perilously low fuel reserves and almost no hope of making it home, Stewart and his crew decided nevertheless to push on across the Mediterranean. The members of the crew began to pray. The radio operator tuned in the Allied radio network, and crackling over the radio came the words of a song they had never before heard, "Coming In on a Wing and a Prayer." The crew looked at each other incredulously. Was this song meant for them? Stewart recalled that they looked around anxiously, expecting to see angels surrounding them. Utah Man did exactly what the song described. They came in on a wing and a prayer, landing safely after fourteen hours of unrelenting crisis.

While Jesus was hanging on the cross he prayed. When my son was found unconscious in a swimming pool my wife prayed. When my friends' plane crashed in the Bering Sea they prayed. Prayer puts crisis where it belongs: in God's hands.

Today's Prayer

Dear God, hear my cry today! Take all my crises, today and tomorrow. Help me to let go and trust you with every detail in my life. Thank you for always being there when I need you most. Let those who hesitate to call on you know they can always count on you. Amen

Growing in Prayer

Memorize this poem, which I have repeated hundreds of times:

At the heart of the cyclone tearing the sky,
flinging the clouds and towers by,
There is a place of peaceful calm.
So here in the world of mortal things,
I have a place where my spirit sings.
It is the hollow of God's hand.

Edwin Markum

Chapter 21

Prayer and Self-worth

———◆———

Keep me as the apple of your eye.
Psalm 17:8 NIV

We go to God,
expecting him to show us all our flaws,
Our face reflecting emptiness
that deep within us gnaws.
God holds a mirror for us
and we behold our face,
Not scarred with sin, as we had feared,
But bathed in love and grace.

21

*L*yle and Nola walked through the science museum, pausing to try several of the displays.

"Here," said Lyle, pointing to a display where two chairs sat facing a two-way mirror between them. "Let's see how this works," he suggested.

The two friends sat down facing each other. They read the directions, looked straight ahead, and began turning knobs to adjust the light level on each side of the mirror.

"Oh, wow!" exclaimed Nola, looking disbelievingly at the image in the mirror.

"What do you see?" Lyle asked.

"With the light on my side fully on, I see just myself," Nola began, "but . . . but when I turn the light on my side down a little and you turn the light on your side of the mirror up, I see you in me. I see your image on my face!" She smiled. "This is wonderful."

"Yes, it is," agreed Lyle, "to see the image of love looking back at you. They should call this display 'Prayer.' "

"What do you mean?" asked Nola.

"Prayer is a little like this two-way mirror," Lyle said. "We so often turn the light up on ourselves and see only our flaws."

"I know just what you mean," sighed Nola.

"But God looks at us through the light of love and sees our great value," countered Lyle, "and when we talk to God through prayer God helps us turn down the light on ourselves and brings up the light on his love. Then we can begin to see what God sees in us—the reflection of his love."

"And I'll bet we see something else," Nola suggested. "We see the joy on both sides."

———————◆———————

Prayer isn't just talking. Prayer is a two-way conversation. When we listen as we pray, God lets us know how valuable we are. God uses prayer to help us develop a sense of our own worth.

You and I were created in the image of God. That means we are treasures. The challenge you and I face is believing that we are valuable. People often say hurtful things to one another. It's hard to maintain a sense of self-worth when someone tells us, however subtly, that we are worthless, or when we think we haven't met our own or other's expectations. It's hard to develop a sense of our own worth when we see images every day of people who seem to be smarter, more athletic, more attractive, more sophisticated, more powerful, or wealthier than we are. And it's hard to believe in our own value when we face our own real faults and failures every day. Shame suffocates us. We get down on ourselves and often we end up tearing others down as well. When we don't believe we are of value we don't believe God values us either.

Prayer corrects that lie by helping us see ourselves through God's loving eyes. God is madly in love with us. Prayer helps us understand that God valued us enough to send his one and only Son, Jesus, to die for us, so that we could be the loving people God created us to be.

Oliver Wendell Holmes had a clear sense of his own worth. He once attended a meeting in which he was the shortest man present. "Dr. Holmes," quipped a friend, "I should think you feel rather small among us big fellows."

"I do," retorted Holmes. "I feel like a dime among a lot of pennies" (*Chicken Soup for the Soul*, p. 67).

We don't necessarily know the source of Holmes' self worth, but we do know that whether we are aware of it or not, God sees us—the work of his hands—as valuable. The creator of the universe says, "I have called you by my name, you are mine" (Isaiah 43:1c). You are important to God! God chose you.

Prayer helps us believe what God thinks about us, rather than what anyone else thinks about us. Prayer also helps us see more clearly the worth of other people. It is difficult to earnestly pray for someone and, at the same time, believe that person has little worth. Prayer helps us see friends, family, and acquaintances through God's eyes. And sharing that God-given perspective helps others grow into the worth-filled creatures God made all of us to be.

―――――◆―――――

Today's Prayer

Dear God, thank you that you value me. Fill me with your worth. Help me to be a builder of worth in others as long as I live. Let it begin today. Amen

Growing in Prayer

Create a list of people you value most:

_____

_____

_____

_____

Now find a way to tell them how valuable they are!

Chapter 22

Prayer and Health

———◆———

*The prayer offered in faith
will make the sick person well.*
James 5:15 NIV

Prayer is an important part
of the prescription for good health.

22

"Which of you," the Teacher said, "if you were a pilot, would ignore weather reports or navigational beacons, or fail to maintain radio contact with the ground? Would you not endanger your 'flying health' if you did so?

"Which of you, then, would put your own health in danger by ignoring those things meant to guide you to good health, or by failing to maintain contact with God, who can steer you around storms, warn you of turbulence, help you navigate through life, and guide you to your destination?

"Prayer—communicating with 'ground control'—is vital to a healthy life."

———◆———

Prayer is healthy. Scientific research has confirmed that prayer contributes to physical health. To verify this, randomly selected hospital patients were placed in two different groups. Group A members had no one praying for them while Group B members were part of an intentional prayer process. The patients in Group B became healthier faster and recovered more rapidly.

Many nurses, doctors, and other health care workers pray for the people they treat because they are convinced that prayer positively affects health.

Sometimes the effect of prayer on health is dramatic. An emergency room physician was called in late one night on a critical case. By the time he arrived, in fact, the emergency room team had determined that the man whose life they desperately tried to save was dead. He had no pulse. When the doctor arrived, he placed his hands on the patient and silently prayed. Amazingly, the

man, given up for dead, coughed. Over the next five minutes, the entire emergency room team worked together to
stabilize the man and, literally, save his life. Prayer is powerful.

Other times prayer's impact on health takes quieter
forms. My mother asked her family for prayers before her
heart-bypass surgery. This helped calm her and fill her
with a feeling of peace before, during, and after the surgery. When my father and I went into the recovery room,
we found Mom's lips moving as she prayed, "Thank you,
Jesus. Thank you, Jesus." Mom reported that she experienced a positive, peaceful feeling throughout the entire
surgical procedure.

Prayer can also attune us to those things that help
keep our bodies in good health in the first place, things
like positive thoughts and attitudes, sound habits, and
constructive, healthy relationships. Through prayer, God
can give us a "prescription" for building and maintaining
wholeness throughout our entire life.

Praying for health doesn't mean we will never get
sick or experience physical decline. However, prayer puts
us in touch with God, the great physician. God created us
and desires that we be whole. When we pray, God shows
us the way.

Today's Prayer

Dear God, thank you for the gift of health. Give me healthy thoughts, habits, and relationships. Remind me that you are the great physician and that you want me to take care of my whole self. I trust you with all my health needs today. Remind me that in sickness and in health, you are always with me. Amen

Growing in Prayer

Think of one healthy thing you could do for yourself this week. Pray that God will help keep you motivated to accomplish that one thing. Then do it.

Chapter 23

Prayer and Time Management

---◆---

For everything there is a season.
Ecclesiastes 3:1

Is your daily planner a "what" or a "who"?

23

"*I* get so frustrated!" Roger said to his neighbor. "I can't figure out this VCR. It seems the more gadgets they invent to make life easier, the more the gadgets control me!"

"I know what you mean," Lowell agreed. "But I've discovered something that really does make it easier." He grinned at his friend's curious look. "I read the directions."

With a wry smile, Roger inquired, "And if you still can't figure it out?"

"Then I go back to the store and find someone who does," Lowell answered.

"It's just too bad there isn't someone to help us figure out the directions for the rest of life," Roger laughed.

"As a matter of fact, there is," said Lowell. "I always used to feel like my life ran me. My time seemed out of my control."

"I know that feeling," agreed Roger. "So what did you do?"

"Well, I turned to the directions," Lowell answered. "I started going to God in prayer and reading the Bible. I figured the one who created life ought to have some pretty good ideas about how to manage it."

"That sounds really sensible," concluded Roger. Then he smiled and added, "The Bible doesn't have anything to say about VCRs, does it?"

◆

Time is often referred to today as the new money. You've probably even said yourself, "I wish I had more time." The best thing we can do to manage time wisely is to pray. Prayer tunes us in to God's time management system.

My personal prayer every day is for God to help me manage time according to his priority clock. God gives us the time every day to do exactly what he has planned. When we over-commit ourselves or when our daily time schedule gets out of control, we cannot blame God. The problem is that we've been looking at our own watch, not God's.

A friend of mine who had a heart attack told me he was amazed by how quickly he was able to clear his time schedule. I read once that the average person has 36 hours of work piled up, but only 90 minutes of time available to complete it. That time crunch is enough to trigger ulcers and other breakdowns. It's a literal time bomb.

Time is meant to be

*T*reasured prayerfully,

*I*nvested carefully,

*M*anaged excellently,

*E*xpended fruitfully.

I have never visited with a person in the last moments of life who said, "I wish I would have wasted more time." That would be absurd. Time is valuable. Some time management trainers encourage people to view every minute of life the way they would view a million dollars. Both time and money, managed rightly, can produce a tremendous return. That is one reason we would be wise to make prayer our number one time management tool.

There is another reason to manage our time with prayer. God often shows us ways to use our time that we never would have thought of.

At one of our church's annual women's retreats, the women on the prayer team were heading to their cabins to get ready for dinner. As they walked up the hill, another woman approached and passed the group. One of the women on the team walked on a few steps, then felt the urge to turn back to talk to the woman who had just passed. "You look like you could use someone to talk with," she said.

"Well, yes," the second woman answered, with tear-stained eyes. "A friend told me to come look for . . . ," and she gave a name, "but I don't know who she is." The woman from the prayer team, amazed, said, "It's me!" The thirty minutes they spent talking and listening to one another—thirty minutes that were not set aside in the retreat schedule or anyone's appointment book—turned out to be the most meaningful of the weekend for both women.

Make God your time keeper. Time taken to follow God's leading is always time well invested. Prayer helps us align our priorities, plans, purposes, and possibilities with God's.

Today's Prayer

Dear God, my time belongs to you. You gave it to me in the first place. Please take control of my time management. I know you want my time to be treasured prayerfully, invested carefully, managed excellently, and expended fruitfully. That is what I want, too! Amen

Growing in Prayer

Take out your appointment book or calendar right now and pray about each appointment and every commitment. Imagine yourself handing over your schedule to God and allowing God to manage each second, minute, and hour of every day. You will be amazed by what happens.

Chapter 24

Prayer and Imagination

———◆———

No eye has seen, no ear has heard,
no mind has conceived
what God has prepared
for those who love him.
1 Corinthians 2:9 NIV

Prayer transforms "tunnel vision"
into "transcending vision."

24

*G*reg and Sally, both tourists, stood on a point overlooking a canyon. "That's quite a camera bag you carry," remarked Greg to Sally. "What all do you have in there?" "Well, mostly extra lenses, film, and filters," Sally answered.

"Why so many lenses?" inquired Greg. "I just have the one that came with my camera."

"Different lenses help me find and photograph more than my eye sees alone," said Sally. "Here, for instance, a standard lens can't take in the sweep of this canyon, so I use a wide-angle lens. But with my telephoto lens, I found a waterfall springing out from the canyon wall far below us." Bending down, she continued, "And I would use a zoom lens to capture this tiny, fragile wildflower against the rough, weathered rock we're standing on."

"So you use these lenses to extend your vision," said Greg, "to see from a new perspective."

"Yes," Sally nodded. "You know, since I've had these lenses, I find myself looking for new ways to see, even when I'm not carrying my camera."

"It sounds like they actually kindle your imagination," said Greg. "I use something similar. I find that prayer ignites my imagination. The lens of prayer enables me to see things in a new way: from God's perspective. Dreams that seem unreachable, abilities that seem too small, possibilities to help in ways that might be overlooked—all these come into focus when I see them from God's perspective through the lens of prayer."

"Then prayer," mused Sally, "really gives you a new way to see."

One of God's most powerful gifts to us is our imagination. We operate most often out of memory or present information. But through the centuries, many people have found ways to get past limitations and obstacles others found insurmountable. Because of imagination we have aircraft, telephones, penicillin, heart surgery, moon walks, and information highways. But imagination is not the sole province of scientists or inventors. Imagination is a necessity for all of us if we are to meet the challenges of our lives.

Hugh Herr discovered this when he lost both legs in a mountain climbing accident in 1982. Facing the prospect of never climbing again, Hugh envisioned and developed five pairs of specialized climbing "feet" to fit his artificial legs. Hugh's imagination transformed disability into ability and literally helped him climb mountains again.

Prayer unlocks our imagination to help us get past what appear to be limitations and obstacles. Prayer transcends human limitations by helping us see the world from God's perspective, which is limitless. God sees how the impossible can become possible. God imagines the unimaginable. God's greatness no one can comprehend, yet through prayer-inspired imagination, we can catch a glimpse of it. This is exactly where breakthrough thinking and inspired ideas are born. God is greatly pleased when we use the gift of imagination. Heaven applauds when we capture transforming ideas and unlock discovery and innovation.

For some people, sitting quietly in prayerful, expectant meditation may be the way they best hear God's inspiration. For others, inspiration comes most easily when they are walking, or waxing the car, or dusting the furniture, freeing the thinking part of the brain, to "brainstorm" with God and listen to what God is saying.

One of my personal prayers is:

"Dear God, please ignite my imagination today. I am confident that, through you, I will see more than I ever thought I could see, hear more than I imagined I could ever hear, experience more than I ever believed I would, and enjoy life more than I ever dreamed I could. Thank you. Amen."

Every morning when I exercise, I start out by stretching my muscles. This helps me warm up so that I get the most out of my exercise. But stretching just muscles is not enough. My mind must be stretched as well. Through prayer we can warm up our minds so that we will get the most out of life today, tomorrow, and forever.

———————◆———————

Today's Prayer

Dear God, thank you for my imagination. Use it to expand every part of my life, so that I can live what you called the "abundant life." I don't want to miss anything that you intended for me to see. Amen

Growing in Prayer

Go to a playground when it is filled with children. Observe their imaginations at work. Record what you learn. Make return visits when you need to keep your imagination stimulated.

Chapter 25

Prayer and Anger

———◆———

Do not let the sun go down on your anger.
Ephesians 4:26

God can take our "AAAUGHH!" and turn
*A*nger into
*A*cceptable
*A*ction
*U*nder
*G*od's
*H*ealing
*H*ands

25

"Which of you," the Teacher said, "would want a child to pick up and hold on to a piece of broken glass? Would you not ask the child to carefully throw the glass away, or to give the glass to you to dispose of properly?

"How much more, then, does our heavenly Father desire that we not hold on to anger, which is as dangerous as broken glass. Pray and ask God to help you drop the anger "into the trash." And if you cannot let go, place the anger, through prayer, in God's hands and trust God to dispose of it."

———————◆———————

Not all anger is bad. Using controlled anger against destructive forces can have positive results when it motivates us to find excellent solutions. Some time ago a mother lost her child when a drunken driver swerved over the center line, causing a fatal head-on collision. This mother, with God's help, was able to channel her anger. She organized Mothers Against Drunk Drivers (MADD). This organization has provided comfort for families and friends of thousands of people who have been killed by drunk drivers. In many states it has helped shape stricter legislation about drunk driving offenses.

This positive result came from one woman's positive use of anger. Uncontrolled anger, however, only makes a problem more severe. Uncontrolled anger seeks to harm another.

All anger needs expression, and prayer helps us appropriately handle anger. That is why we need to channel anger through prayer.

The challenge to us, though, is that anger can take away our desire to pray. Anger can rob us of reason so that we lose sight of the power of prayer to heal. Anger can also be addictive and hard to let go of. When we take our anger to God we must let it go, and this can be difficult to do. Sometimes anger makes us feel a sense of shame, so we are embarrassed to come before God. For these and other reasons, we often feel we cannot pray when we are angry.

But remember, God doesn't love us any less when we are angry. In fact, God is still "mad about you" even when you are mad at him! God always encourages us to give our anger to him, even if it is God that we are angry with. God invites us to come with all of our anger and place it in his hands.

The anger that we refuse to pray about will hurt us. In earlier times, loggers would haul logs out of the woods to a landing on a riverbank. From there the logs could be floated down the river to a mill where they were cut into useful lumber. Log jams on the river could be treacherous, so agile lumberjacks would jump from one log to another, driving the logs downriver to keep them from jamming along the way.

Anger that we hold on to, like uncontrolled logs, will "jam" within us and turn into bitterness, rage, self-pity, depression, and other self-destructive emotions. Anger held inside will cause physical, emotional, and spiritual problems. Unbridled anger within us can lead to violence and even early death.

Prayer is a river wide enough to safely carry our anger to the place where God can transform it, producing useful, healthy, and positive results.

Today's Prayer

Dear God, take my anger about _____ and use it for powerful good. Forgive me for trying to handle anger on my own. I am grateful that you care about not only my happiness but about my anger as well. Amen

Growing in Prayer

Identify one person or situation that you feel anger toward and write a prayer letter to God. (No postage required. God will hand-deliver it!)

Chapter 26

Prayer and Money

———◆———

*Where your treasure is,
there your heart will be also.*
Matthew 6:21

Praying about your finances
gives you your money's worth.

26

"Why is that violinist standing up and just playing one note?" the student asked the teacher.

"That person is the concertmaster," explained the teacher. "She is giving the rest of the orchestra a pitch—a concert A. Now you can hear them all tuning their own instruments to match her note. Imagine," the teacher asked, "what the music would sound like if all the instruments were not in tune."

"That would sound terrible," the student responded.

"That's right," the teacher continued. "So for the orchestra to be in harmony, all the instruments must be in tune with the concertmaster."

As the teacher huddled with the student in hushed conversation, one of the people seated behind them whispered to the friend seated next to him, "I had to learn that same principle with my checkbook recently."

"What do you mean?" the friend asked.

"Well," the man continued, "I discovered it wasn't in harmony with what God desired."

"But how could you tell? Since you're in business for yourself," his friend said, "your income isn't even steady."

"True," the man acknowledged, "and that's why it's so important for me to keep my heart in tune with God's. When I pray, God helps me know what's of value. God gives me a note to tune to, if you will. Then whether I'm working with a little or a lot, all of my assets can work in harmony."

Your checkbook is an excellent prayer journal. God has given us everything we have and wants us to manage all our resources prayerfully. Prayer helps us understand God's thoughts about money. Your checkbook helps you see how you have responded to God's thoughts about money. What we spend our money on matters to us, but it matters even more to God.

Recently I visited a friend of a former billionaire. Over the last ten years, this rich man has lost most of his fortune. But he commented about money, "The only money that ever gave me any pleasure was the money I gave away."

God is even more generous than this billionaire was. So giving money away in God's name can bring us tremendous satisfaction. After all, giving is what God does. "God so loved the world that he gave . . ." (John 3:16).

God desires responsible money management even more than we do, but for many people money is a problem. Either they have too little, so they get mad at God for not caring about their needs, or they have too much, so they think they have everything they need to make it on their own and begin to believe they don't need God. If we have money problems, it makes sense to pray about them because no one is wise enough or knowledgeable enough to handle money—either a little or a lot—without God's guidance.

The good news is that God promised that all our needs would be supplied—not necessarily all our *wants*, but all our *needs*. When I was ready to pack up my young family of four and move to Amarillo, Texas, for my seminary internship, I had no idea how we could survive on a monthly salary of $500. Rent alone was going to be over $400, and then there would be food, gasoline, and other expenses. My wife and I had also made a $100-per-week commitment to our church building fund. It was a very scary time in my life, and I prayed. Shortly before we loaded the moving truck, the phone rang. A close friend from college called to tell me he had been praying for me that day. He said that during his prayer time, God told him to call me and tell me that he was going to pay for my family's apartment rent during our entire internship. I was stunned! My wife and I were overwhelmed when we realized how God had answered our prayers. Throughout the internship year, God continued to provide for everything we needed. It was amazing to see. We learned firsthand that prayer and money are inseparable.

Whether you need money, or you need to give money away, pray. Even the currency we use has "In God We Trust" printed on it. Trust in God—and pray.

Today's Prayer

Dear God, thank you for the money you have provided. Help me to manage money in the way you intended. Make me gracious in receiving and generous in giving of everything you supply, whether it is a little or a lot. Thank you. Amen

Growing in Prayer

Make a chart like the one below. Be specific.

I have these needs:	I have these assets:
Everything belongs to God	

Memorize this and repeat it daily:

"My God will supply all my needs according to God's unlimited resources."

Chapter 27

Prayer and Loneliness

——◆——

I am with you always.
Matthew 28:20

Prayer builds a bridge
that spans our loneliness.
Across that bridge God calls others to us,
us to others,
and everyone to him.

27

"*I*'m sure glad somebody built this bridge," said Cynthia to Audrey, as the two hiked back to their campsite. "I'd hate to have to cross this gully in the dark."

"A lot of people probably do try to cross the gully, not knowing that the bridge is here," Audrey remarked. "I'm glad you knew where it was."

Stopping to look down into the rocky ravine, Cynthia observed, "This gully reminds me of what happened to me when I first moved out here, away from everything I knew. I felt so empty and lonely. I didn't know how to begin to fill up the hole I felt inside me. I prayed about it, and you know what?"

"God filled the hole?" ventured Audrey.

"No, God didn't replace what I'd left behind. I'll always miss the people I left back home. But through prayer God helped me find a bridge, anchored in his love. Prayer connected me with God, and I saw that God was there, already reaching to span my loneliness."

"We're certainly glad God led you to help in our program," said Audrey. "You've brought God's joy to a lot of young people, and started them across bridges of their own."

"No one has to remain in that chasm of loneliness," emphasized Cynthia, "when God is there to help them bridge the gap."

———◆———

Loneliness cannot last in the face of God's compelling presence. When we pray, we are never alone.

Mom and Dad were married for over 50 years. They were together as much as possible. But when Dad died,

Mom became very lonely. Often when I visited her, she
would comment that during her loneliest moments she
would pray. While praying, she felt the presence of God
and her loneliness was often transformed into companionship with God. God's companionship is the antidote to
loneliness.

Andy battled terrible loneliness after his divorce. His
wife and small children left the state to start a new life.
There were hours when Andy felt so lonely he even con-
sidered suicide. Then one night he fell to his knees and
cried out for God to help him. A strange, warm presence
touched him on the shoulder. Andy experienced the power of prayer that helped him deal with his painful loneliness.

Jesus knows how loneliness feels. He encountered
the depths of loneliness on the night he was alone praying
in the garden, only minutes before his arrest. Jesus was so
lonely that he begged his friends to stay awake and be
with him. They fell asleep when Jesus needed them most,
but God stayed with him. And even though Jesus endured
the depths of loneliness, crying out from the cross "My
God, why have you forsaken me?" (Matthew 27:46b NIV),
he knew that God was very near to him. Finally he cried,
"Father, into your hands I commit my spirit" (Luke 23:46a
NIV). God not only stayed awake. God stuck with him
through the entire betrayal, arrest, trial, sentencing, death,
and resurrection.

Prayer connects us to all of God's resources for han-
dling loneliness. Certainly God comes to us in spirit, but
God also comes to us through real people. I love the story
about the little girl who moved into a new home where
for the first time she had her own large bedroom. In the
middle of the night she woke up feeling very lonely, so
she got up and ran into her mommy and daddy's bedroom
and crawled into bed with them. The little girl told her
parents that she felt lonely. They said, "You aren't alone.
God is there with you."

But the little girl protested, "I need someone with skin on."

When we pray, God comes "with skin on," naturally, through friendly companionship with people. God also comes supernaturally with his warm, tender, compassionate, friendly Spirit. The Bible refers to this as the Holy Spirit. Jesus promised that when he physically ascended into heaven, a comforter—the Holy Spirit—would come. For anyone who is lonely today, that certainly is a comforting thought. Put the welcome mat out today.

Today's Prayer

Dear God, when I am lonely, I know you are with me because you promised that you would be. Please transform my loneliness into companionship. Thank you that I can always count on your presence! Amen

Growing in Prayer

Volunteer your service in a church, hospital, school, or other place of need. There are needs that even people who can't leave their homes can fill. Offering yourself to help others does amazing things to ease loneliness and build bridges.

Chapter 28

Prayer and Fear

Do not fear, for I have redeemed you;
I have called you by name,
you are mine.
Isaiah 43:1

Fear blinds us from seeing God.
Faith binds us to a seeing God!

28

"Which of you," the Teacher said, "when boating on a lake far from shore and discovering a leak in your canoe, would either sit staring at the leak and allow your boat to fill, or pretend there was no leak and allow so much water to enter that it swamped the canoe? Would you not rather paddle to shore and find help so that you might put your canoe back in the water?

"So it is with fear. Fear is as insidious and unremitting as a leak in a boat. We should neither focus solely on fear nor pretend that it doesn't exist, but head to shore and take our fear to God in prayer. God can help us do what is needed to deal with the fear so that we can securely put our boat back in the water."

———————◆———————

Fear gives us the footwear to run to God. When we are filled with fear, the first thing we need to do is pray. When we pray, we become connected to God. We cannot have a faith thought and a fear thought at the same time, so when God fills us with faith, we no longer feel afraid.

A friend laughingly admitted that fear had once played a big part in her own life. "When my husband was in the service, he frequently had to be away from home for days or weeks at a time. In the early days of our marriage, I resorted to some pretty silly things out of fear of staying alone. I put newspaper down the hallway and set up empty cans in front of the door so I could hear if anybody tried to break in. What I would have done if anyone had broken in, I don't know. Even with the house booby-trapped, I didn't feel secure. In fact, I was the one trapped in fear. When our first child was born, that only gave me one more reason to worry whenever I had to stay alone.

"After six years my husband left the service, only to take a civilian job that meant he had to be away from home for months instead of weeks. On the first night of a six-month separation, I stood at the front door and, together with God, took a look at my fear. I knew I had to make a choice. Tin cans and newspapers couldn't protect us. That was literally rubbish. Even locks couldn't ensure our safety. Only God could truly keep us safe and secure. I could spend six months, either living in fear or living in faith.

"That night I turned to God. As I locked each door, I thanked God for being our shield and defense. I told God I trusted him to be our protector. That night and every night thereafter I prayed and then slept soundly, knowing we were not alone in the house but surrounded by the strength and faithfulness of God. Now I know that whenever I am tempted to fear, the best thing I can do is pray."

What is your greatest fear today? Is it public speaking, or losing your job, or violence, or death? Whatever it is, remember your fear is not more powerful than God. God has faced and overcome everything we fear.

Prayer enables us to believe that fear doesn't have the final say. God does. Prayer gives us the courage to face our fear.

If you knew the final score of a football game before you played it and knew that you would win, you could play with abandon. Prayer provides the same confidence. We know that no matter what happens, God has already won. Through God we are a part of the winning team.

Carol Schuller, daughter of Robert Schuller, lay in a pool of her own blood after being thrown from a motorcycle. She hovered between life and death from her serious loss of blood. Finally Carol's condition was stabilized, but her damaged leg had to be amputated. Fear of the unknown gripped the entire Schuller family. After months of healing and rehabilitation, Carol spoke about her experience. She said the most important discovery she made was that even though she would never walk on two legs again, it didn't matter. How she walked wasn't important. What mattered was the One with whom she walked.

That's it! The answer to fear is faith in Jesus Christ. The way to connect with Christ is through prayer. Welcome Christ into your fear today and let him transform your debilitating fear into exhilarating faith.

Today's Prayer

Dear God, take my fears today and replace them with faith. I believe that fear has no power over me because you are my Savior. I love you. Amen

Growing in Prayer

Think about your greatest fear today. Write it down.

_____

_____

Now, boldly write over that fear the word "faith"!

Chapter 29

Prayer and Forgiveness

———◆———

Forgive me my sins, as I forgive others.
Matthew 6:12, paraphrase

Through prayer God can remind us that
unforgiveness became won forgiveness,
and became ours, through Jesus.

29

*C*onsider a solar water heater in which sunlight heats water piped through collectors. The heated water is then pumped into a storage tank and from there into the building. This simple system usually functions well but under certain extremes there can be problems.

Intense sunlight can heat water to a temperature too high to use safely. So the system needs a mixer valve to add enough cool water to the hot water to bring the mixture to a safe temperature. Conversely, when the outside air temperature is very low, the water in the outside pipes may freeze. So warm water from the storage tank must be pumped to the collectors to protect the pipes from rupturing. Either way, water that is just the right temperature is pumped into the building.

Likewise, when someone hurts us, we may feel frustration, bitterness, anger, grief, shock, pain, distrust, disbelief, and a host of other emotions. Prayer acts like a mixer valve. God can take our heat—our anger, frustration, resentment—and mix it with his mercy, compassion, and wisdom so that we and others, aren't burned by what we think or do or say. Likewise, when we feel the numbing cold of distrust, grief, or pain, God can warm us with his reservoir of grace, strength, and love. In either case, through prayer we ultimately receive the grace to forgive.

———◆———

The way to forgiveness is through prayer. Jesus prayed for those who nailed him to the cross, "Father, forgive them. . . ." (Luke 23:34 NIV).

David Lee Thompson, a convicted child molester, was interviewed on television. The interviewers asked how he was finally caught and arrested. David became very quiet. Then he told about a little girl he had molested. He had physically hurt her, but the little girl looked into his eyes and pleaded, "Mister, can I pray for you that God would forgive you?"

These words shocked David to the core of his being. That had never happened to him before. For the first time in his life, he felt remorse and shame. This, he said, was the beginning of the end of his horrible life of abuse.

Forgiveness is an act, not a feeling. We might feel like retaliating because we are hurt, but we can decide instead to forgive. Choosing to forgive in spite of our feelings is costly. As someone aptly put it, "There are no 'discount' pardons."

Forgiveness is powerful. Indeed, it is because of the power of God's forgiveness that we can become forgiving people in the first place. And again, whether we forgive or are the ones forgiven, we find that every act of forgiveness changes us. Forgiveness makes us stronger by making our hearts tender and our faith tougher.

But where do we find the courage to ask for forgiveness, or the strength to choose to forgive? That strength comes from God, and we can ask for and find that strength through prayer. God is eager to help us choose to forgive and to go on living in the power of that choice—to *forget.*

God said, " . . . for I will forgive their iniquity, and remember their sin no more" (Jeremiah 31:34b). My wife and I have a "24-hour promise." When one of us does something wrong and asks for forgiveness, after twenty-four hours we can never bring it up again. This helps us actually practice forgiving and forgetting. Through prayer we are able to keep our twenty-four-hour promise.

I love the story of the two elderly gentlemen who were discussing heaven. One man suggested, "Let's make a promise to each other tonight. The first one to die will ask God what the worst sin in each of our lives has been and come back to tell the other." They agreed to the idea. A short time later one of the men died. Only days after that, he came back to visit his friend, as he promised. His friend welcomed him back and asked, "Well, what did God say my worst sin was?" The reply was, "God told me he couldn't remember." When we pray for forgiveness, God answers that prayer and remembers our sins no more.

Decide to forgive and forget right now. Through prayer it is possible. Prayer is the pathway to forgiving and forgetting.

◆

Today's Prayer

Dear God, forgive me all my sins as I forgive those who have sinned against me. Help me never to miss the joy of living by hanging on to others' faults and failures. Thank you for giving me forgetfulness when it comes to my own failures, as well as the failure of others. Amen

Growing in Prayer

Name someone you need to forgive today.

_____

Now pray: "God, please help me forgive and forget it! Amen."

Chapter 30

Prayer and Love

———◆———

And the greatest of these is love.
1 Corinthians 13:13

True love is "communicable" through prayer.

30

"And this is what I picked up for my children," Anita said to the passenger in the seat next to hers. She held up a group of colored wooden rectangles connected by a strap. Holding the top rectangle in her hand, she let the others fall in a cascade of colors. Then she gathered the rectangles again, holding what had been the bottom one, and let the remaining blocks fall. This time the pattern of colors changed as the rectangles tumbled, revealing their opposite sides.

"Oh, a Jacob's ladder," smiled Herb. "I had one of those when I was a kid. In fact," he added, "I still have it in a box at home."

"Maybe I should've bought one for myself. I've been playing with this one for hours, enjoying it and trying to understand how it works," Anita admitted.

"Toys often use and illustrate important principles," Herb observed. "I found something else that works a little like a Jacob's ladder."

"What's that?" inquired Anita.

"Prayer," Herb answered. "Sometimes I come to God, confused or frustrated or offended by what other people have done or said. The only pattern I know is the side of them I can see. But I've found that, when I lift those people to God in prayer, God can show me another side—how he sees them—and show me a new pattern for loving them."

Prayer builds love into our lives. To pray is to communicate with God. To communicate is "to cause another or others to partake of or share in" (*Funk and Wagnall's*

Dictionary [New York: Reader's Digest, 1966]). So when we pray, we "partake of" or plug into God's authentic, unconditional, non-judgmental love. We experience God's love up close. These encounters with love can shape our attitudes and influence our actions.

To communicate also means "to convey knowledge of, as one's thoughts." All of us have been around negative, judgmental people. We all know those thoughts. Prayer helps us relate to other people in a more loving way by conveying to us God's thoughts about them. This helps us make our mistakes on the side of love, not judgment.

To communicate is also to "exchange thought or knowledge." Both meanings of the word *exchange* can be found in prayer. Through prayer we can come to know God's thoughts and exchange judgmental thoughts for the knowledge of transforming love.

It is not possible to pray for someone regularly and treat them shabbily. When we pray, we place the people we pray for in God's hands. God then helps us begin to love one another as he intended us to love.

Two years ago I was really struggling to love some people who had hurt me deeply. The hurt was so pervasive that it consumed most of my thoughts. At night I would often wake up thinking about what those people did to me. Then I chose to spend an entire hour in prayer for these people. I asked God to help me have an attitude of love and a desire for helping, not harming, the ones who hurt me.

It worked. When I became more loving, so did they! Of course, things don't always turn out so happily, but once again I was reminded how a decision to love can change everything, and that love is a decision. Prayer helps all of us decide to love, even when we don't feel like loving.

If we are honest, some people are harder to love than others. In fact, there are people who send our emotions flip-flopping every time we see them. God tells us, however, to love even our enemies. With God's help, it is possible for love to win. The Bible places the love challenge before us: "Beloved, let us love one another. because love is from God; everyone who loves is born of God and knows God. Whoever does not love does not know God, for God is love" (1 John 4:7-8).

God's challenge to love is amazingly clear. It is not easy to do, though. So let's turn to God and ask for the grace to love. And then let's love—unconditionally, non-judgmentally, extravagantly—today, tomorrow, and forever!

Today's Prayer

Dear God, because you first loved me, I can and will love others. Fill my life with your powerful love and love this world through me. I love you! Amen

Growing in Prayer

Slowly read from the Bible 1 Corinthians 13. Write a definition of love using your own words.

Chapter 31

Prayer and Happiness

———◆———

Blessed are those who hunger and thirst for righteousness, for they will be filled.
Matthew 5:6

Life's Laundering Instructions:
To retain true happiness, add prayer.

31

"*I*s it just my imagination, or do you have a lot of green clothes, Keith?" his mother asked as they folded laundry together on his first night home from college.

"Well," Keith began, "you know that great jade green shirt that I bought last fall: every time I washed it, it faded. After the first few times—after it turned all my socks green—I figured it would stop fading, but it didn't. Why not, Mom?"

"Well," explained his mother, "what keeps a dye from fading is the bond between the fabric and the particular kind of dye. Sometimes a manufacturer will use a dye that isn't color-fast, or use a dye that doesn't bind to the particular kind of fabric used. Then washing, bleach, sunlight, rubbing, or even perspiration can cause the dye to fade."

"Boy, that's kind of a rip-off," Keith shook his head. "I'll have to shop more carefully, I guess."

"You know," put in Keith's father, setting down his cup thoughtfully, "I learned something of the same sort this past year. I had the same problem with happiness that you had with your shirt: it always seemed to fade away. Even the promotion I got this year didn't seem to bring any great, lasting changes in how I felt."

"So . . . , what does bring you happiness that doesn't wash away, Dad?" inquired Keith, intrigued.

"Not what, but who," replied his father. "I've finally gotten serious about praying, and I've discovered that God is the only source of happiness that lasts. What the world passes off as happiness—money, influence, possessions, vacations—fades away after just a few washings in reality." He paused. "God brings happiness that doesn't fade."

"Wow, I just learned two new things," said Keith. "Always check the label—and the only color-fast happiness comes from God."

———————◆———————

One of the things we learn from a consistent prayer life is that happiness is not circumstantial. Happiness is the certainty of Jesus Christ. Jesus took care of all the forces, farces, and faces that try to destroy us. Through the life, death, and resurrection of Jesus, the victory has been secured. Because of what Jesus did, no matter what happens to us we are on the winning team.

Have you ever watched a victory celebration? It's fun to watch winners because they overflow with happiness. One afternoon, a year after I arrived in Phoenix, the local high school football coach called me and invited me to speak to the team before a game. He told me they had not won a single game in the school's history. In fact, the "pep rallies" had become "pep-less follies."

I accepted the invitation, wondering what I was going to say. When I arrived, the team was sitting with their heads down. The local newspaper predicted that they would lose that night's game 57 to 0, the same score as the previous year. My talk centered around Vince Lombardi's experience of taking a losing team and developing it into world champions. I used a verse from the Bible on encouragement as well: " . . . With God all things are possible" (Matthew 19:26b NIV).

Then I had the team members join hands and pray. Our prayer was that the players would be united and focus on the "winner of winners," Jesus Christ. We didn't pray to win the game; we prayed to play like winners. As the team burst out of the locker room and onto the field that night, they had a winning spirit etched in their minds and on their hearts.

The outcome of the game was remarkable: it ended in a victory for them; the first win in their history. That wasn't the most important thing that happened, though. Following that victory, a contagious confidence swept through the entire student body. Certainly not all of the school's problems were solved, but the attitude of the students was positively affected. They became winners.

Following that game, I worked with the football team, cheerleaders, and spirit squad for nearly three years as team chaplain. Even today, students call and visit me when a tragedy or a triumph has touched their lives because they have want me to pray with them. What began as an opportunity to boost some sagging spirits turned into a powerful witness that true and lasting happiness, even when we don't win, comes through a relationship with God. And a relationship with God is only a prayer away!

---◆---

Today's Prayer

Dear God, I thank you that you will fill my life with happiness while I am living and give my life a "happy ending," no matter what path life and death will take me. Amen

Growing in Prayer

Remember the happiest day of your life. Relive it in your imagination and offer a prayer of thanks for it.